German

Your Complete Guide For German Language Learning

Including

German Grammar Workbook

German Phrasebook

German Short Stories for Beginners

+

Audio Learning

Table of Contents

Introduction

Your professional outlook may require that you need to learn German, and let's face it: with knowledge of the German language, you have more possibilities, - this can be of a professional nature, or for travel and social reasons. In fact, German is especially geared toward professionals as a foreign language of choice with rising tendencies. German, for instance, is the second most important language for science and scientific research. In Europe, professional German teachers are not only highly respected but are paid above-average salaries. In terms of communication and technology worldwide, - Germany is ranked sixth, and when it comes to trade, Germany has the fourth largest economy. Therefore, by learning to speak and understand the German language, you can definitely expand your career. German pensioners and travelers are spending more than any other European country on travel and accommodation. Furthermore, if you interact with Germans, (professionally or socially), your chance of forging a meaningful personal relationship is infinitely higher if you can communicate with them in German.

Moreover, German is a cultural language that can give you access to German literature, art, music and philosophy. So, having knowledge of the German language makes absolute sense, and this material gives you the tools to advance your skills quickly and securely. Just follow the content step-by-step, starting with the basics.

Our aim is to provide students with learning tools they can use to learn German in a reasonable short time and to speak German fluently and with confidence.

What You can Expect from this Book

This book will provide you with various summaries of the fundamentals of the language.

Part 1: Learning the German Language Guide

The first part is a working textbook where you learn the fundamentals of the language, the pronunciation., the foundation of the language and grammar.

The book is structured in a practical way, so you can get familiar with the language step-by-step and at your own pace. You get to understand the German alphabet, and valuable lessons to acquaint yourself with the pronunciation.

This book will show you new and holistic learning approaches, the best way to implement you acquired skills and it will explain the synchronic linguistics in a practical way.

Part 2: Practical and Accelerated Learning Methods

The "**accelerated learning methods**" will guide you through a step-by-step process of new and proven methods used in accredited German language schools that will enable you to learn the pillars of the language as well as the practical applications. You will improve your German step-by-step using professional methods. This book also includes many practical exercises and important tips for learners that you can use as you advance with the learning material.

Part 3: Short Stories for Language Students

In the third part of this book, you can read 15 German short stories with English parallel text designed for language learners. Each short story is accompanied with a vocabulary section, learning question and audio.

Each story comes with its own downloadable audio mp4 file to compare your understanding of the text and improve your pronunciation.

This book can be considered as a comprehensive toolkit for learners, especially if you happened to be in a German speaking environment. This book also covers the basics of the grammatical structure, practical tips and exercises. These are all important tools designed to improve your language skills considerably.

Part 4 Modern German Phrasebook

In this realistic phrasebook you'll be able to learn the language through **700 realistic and common German phrases and expression** for travelers and students so you can acquire a practical grasp of the language and developing skills to express yourself in a natural way just as a German native speaker does. This book provides essential and realistic phrases to achieve, fluency and competency in German. In a word, this book aims to be a compact learning guide which includes some new and unusual learning techniques, but at the same time you can use this book as a resource that you can use in your everyday communication when speaking with Germans.

LEARNING
THE
GERMAN LANGUAGE
GUIDE
ACADEMY DER SPRACHCLUB
Language
Starter
Book

Part 1

Learning the German Language

German Words

Spelling and Pronunciation

German spelling and pronunciation aren't as troublesome as one might think, because most vowels and consonants are related to the English language. You basically spell exactly what you hear, and once you get used and understand the sounds of German letters, it becomes easy and natural to spell the language. However, it is important to learn how to pronounce the words clearly and correctly so you can understand at once what is said when someone speaks to you in German.

Learning the proper pronunciation starts by actively practicing the pronunciation of letters. Once you have learned how specific letters or combinations of letters are pronounced, you should be able to speak with confidence and say almost all words correctly. You will find many examples and short lessons to practice on what you have learned.

The German Alphabet - Consonants and Vowels

The German language uses the 26 - letter Latin alphabet which is also used in English, but in German each letter either has a different name, is unique or is pronounced differently. German also has four additional distinct letter sounds which will be explained by practical examples. Some letters may be challenging to English speakers as there is no parallel sound in English.

Before we get into learning the consonants and vowels let's take a quick glance at this overview of the alphabet and pronunciation:

A (a) /ɑ:/Long 'a' as 'a' in 'father' (ah).
B (be) /be:/ Pronounced like 'p' when at the end of a word
C (ce) /tse:/ See combination letter forms; without a following 'h': before 'e', 'i', 'y', 'ä', 'ö' like the German letter 'z' else like 'k'
D (de) /de:/ Pronounced like 't' when at the end of a word; slightly more "dental"
E (e) /e:/ Long 'e' as 'a' in 'late' (ay) without (!) the (y). Short 'e' as 'e' in 'pet'. In "unstressed" syllables like 'a' in 'about' or 'e' in 'garden'

F (ef) /ɛf/

G (ge) /ge:/ Pronounced like 'g' in 'get'; pronounced like 'k' when at the end of a word; pronounced like 'ich'-sound (see below) in the suffix '-ig' at the end of words

H (ha) /hɑ:/ like 'h' in house, only at the beginning of words or a syllable before 'a', 'i', 'o', 'u', 'y', 'ä', 'ö', 'ü' (only if these vowels don't belong to a suffix), else silent

I (i) /i:/ Long 'i' as 'e' in 'seen' (ee); short 'i' as 'i' in 'pit'

J (jot) /jot/ Pronounced like 'y' in 'yard'

K (ka) /kɑ:/

L (el) /ɛl/ Slightly more "dental"

M (em) /ɛm/

N (en) /ɛn/ Slightly more "dental"; before 'a', 'i', 'o', 'u', 'y', 'ä', 'ö', 'ü' (only if these vowels don't belong to a suffix)

O (o) /o:/ Long 'o' as 'o' in 'open' (oh), there is no movement in the sound as in the English equivalent. Short 'o' as 'o' in 'pot'

P (pe) /pe:/

Q (ku) /ku:/ Pronounced like 'k'; only occurs in the combination 'qu', which is pronounced like 'kv' not like 'kw'

R (er) /ɛʀ/ trilled with the front or back of the tongue, depending on area (see below)

S (es) /ɛs/ In Germany, pronounced like the English 'z'; pronounced like 's' in 'sound' when at the end of a word, after consonants (except 'l', 'm', 'n', ng') and before consonants; in Austria, pronounced like 'z' only when it appears between two vowels, pronounced like 's' otherwise. Pronounced like 'sh' in the beginning of a word before 'p' or 't'

T (te) /te:/ Slightly more "dental"

U (u) /uː/ Long 'u' as 'oo' in 'moon' (oo); short 'u' as 'u' in 'put'
V (vau) /faʊ/ Pronounced like 'f' when at the end of a word, in the prefixes 'ver-' and 'vor-' and in a few, but often used words - in most cases of Germanic origin-, in general at the beginning of German family and geographical names. In all other cases like 'v'
W (ve) /veː/ Pronounced like 'v'
X (iks) /ɪks/ Pronounced like 'ks'
Y (üpsilon) /ʏpsɪlon/ Pronounced like 'ü' (see below), except in words of English origin, where it is pronounced like in English
Z (zet) /tsɛt/ Pronounced like 'ts'

Our Tips for Pronouncing "Umlaute"

ä, ö, and ü

To pronounce the "ä" sound, say “ay” as in *May* or as in the German word crow: *die Krähe*.

While continuing to spell this sound just tightly round your lips. Look in a mirror and make sure your lips are actually rounded. *Bitte sehr!* The resulting sound is the: **ä** sound. (sounds like to *bed*)

A similar method can be used with the **ü**-sound. The **ü** sound doesn't have a equal in English. Again, while saying the sound, try to round your lips. Then the resulting sound is the **ü**-sound. In case you know how to pronounce **u** in French, it sounds just like the German **ü**

Like any unfamiliar sounds, being able to pronounce the German **ö** and **ü** correctly, can only come with repeated practice!

More About Vowels

Now let's take a look at German vowels. To non-German speaker German vowels probably sound strange and very different, so it is worth studying and practicing them, especially if your native tongue is other than English.

In German there are eight vowels: *a, e, i, o, u,* plus the "mutated vowels", the so-called *Umlaute: ä, ö,* and *ü.*

German vowels and *Umlaute* are all pronounced in a pure and strong way, and unlike in English and most other Germanic languages where vowels tend to be pronounced softer and often as diphthongs.

Also, there is a difference in length:

Vowels can be long or short. When a vowel is followed by a double consonant, for example like double "l" or double "m" they are short, but when a vowel is followed by only one consonant, they are long vowels:

schnell (short) - quick
haben (long) – to have
der Schnee (long) - snow
hell (short) – bright
der Regen (long) – rain

/i/ like in "with" (short) or "feet" (long)
Ich (short) – I

/o/ like in "hot" (short) or "door" (long) *offen* (short) – open *der Ofen* (long) – oven/stove

/u/ like in "bush" (short) or "boot" (long)
(ich) muss (short) – I must
der Kuchen (long) – cake

- **The German *Umlaute* are vowels and can be transcribed as follows:**

ä (a-Umlaut) – ae

ö (b-Umlaut) – oe

ü (u.Umlaut) – ue

Pronunciation: ä like in "head," but with a wide opened mouth:

die Hände – hands

dier Äpfel - apples

Pronunciation: ö like in "burn, heard, sir"

öffnen – to open

die *Köpfe* – heads

Pronunciation: ü like in "Tyrell, new, few"
die Tür – door
über – over/above

- You should know that there's a slight difference in open and closed pronunciation of the *Umaute ä, ö, ü.*

- You might also notice that when trying to imitate the *Umlaute* there is a slight difference in the mouth position of your lips. German pronunciations are more harsh, from round closed to wide open. However, this is something you can improve on and is relatively easy to do by carefully listening to the pronunciations and by imitating those sounds.

- You also have to know that there is a slight difference in open and closed pronunciation of the "Umaute" sounds *ä, ö, ü*. However, this is something you can improve on, once you know the basic sounds and pronunciations of the vowels and by listening carefully to the German pronunciation and by imitating those sounds. You will probably notice that there is a slight difference in the mouth position of your lips. Generally speaking, German pronunciations are more harsh.

Pronouncing Diphthongs

Diphthongs are combinations that consist of at least two vowels in one syllable.

But instead of being pronounced separately, (or in two separate words) the two letters have one sound or pronunciation. A typical example would be the au combination.

Our tip:

The diphthong *au* in German sounds like *OW* as in English “couch”, the "ou" being an English diphthong; the *au* is also part of some German words such as *lauschen,* or *autsch*, which is pronounced almost the same as “couch” in English!)

ai - Pronunciation: Like the vowel sound in English "mine", but more tense and clipped.

oi - Pronunciation: Like the vowel sound in English "coin", but more short, tense, and clipped.

au - Pronunciation: Like the vowel sound in English "house", but slightly more tense and clipped.

Near Cognates

There are words in German which bear almost the same spelling as their English counterpart.

Here are some of the usual spelling conventions used in German: In most German words, the "**c**" in English becomes "**k**".

The "**ou**" in words like "trout" or "mouth" becomes "**au**" in German.

Only a few words in German end in "**-ig**". However "**y**" ending in adjectives like "watery" becomes "- **ig**" in German. The "**y**" ending in nouns like "story" becomes "**-ie**" in German.

-lich is fairly common in German which means "**ly**" ending in nouns like "family" becomes "**-lich**" in German.

The infamous and hard to pronounce "**ch**" is not as difficult as its reputation. It is pronounced like a soft c or soft k. For example, In the word "sechs" (six), the pronunciation is easy for English natives: "zeks". Every time you see "**chs**", it is pronounced like "**ks**" -it's one sound for us, but there are some exceptions like ". Buchregal" (because it's a compound of the words Buch and Regal)

Appreciating the German “Stress”

When learning how to pronounce a word correctly it is important to learn the stress in specific letters.

If you are wondering why there are syllables that are italicized, those are "stressed syllables". The German language does indicate a “stress position” in German words. Although there are actually a few general rules to determine the position of the stressed syllable, there are a many exceptions, which means you will have to memorize the pronunciation of such words by heart.

Learning Nouns and Adjectives

Nouns

The grammatical concept of gender in nouns can be confusing, especially for beginners.

In German all nouns must have a specific gender which means all words, all objects, and all living things are grouped as gender.

German nouns are grouped into three genders:

Masculine - *der,*

Feminine - *die,*

and Neuter - *das.*

To a non-speaking German, the gender choice may seem illogical or random, which it basically is.

However, the genders are easier to learn if you try to distinguish which nouns are which gender.

There are many rules for the advanced student, but experience shows that it's best to learn the gender of a noun when you memorize the noun together with the gender. For example: der Mann, die Frau, das Auto.

These are the most common nouns in masculine, feminine, and neuter form:

Nouns	Nomen	Neuter
English	German	Pronunciation
shelf	das Regal	das re-gahl
Book	das Buch	das bu-ch
paper	das Papier	das pa-peer
house	das Haus	das house
Salt	das Salz	das zalts
insect	das Insekt	das in-zekt
toy	das Spielzeug	das speel-zoyg
program	das Programm	das proh-gram
Telephone	das Telefon	das te-le-fon
Knife	das Messer	das meh-zzer

Nouns	**Nomen**	**Masculine**
English	German	pronunciatiom
man	Der Mann	der man
worker	der Arbeiter	der ar-bey-ter
coffee	der Kaffee	der kaf-ey
pot	der Topf	der to-bf
cupboard	der Schrank	der shrank
check	der Scheck	der shek
pencil	der Bleistift	der bley-shtift
bucket	der Eimer	der Ey-mer

Nouns	**Nomen**	**Feminine**
English	German	Pronunciation
culture	die Kultur	dee kool-toohr
music	die Musik	dee mooh-zeek
camera	die Kamera	dee ca-mera
machine	die Maschine	dee ma-sheen-e
milk	die Milch	dee mi-lch
industry	die Industrie	dee in-dooh-stree
trousers	die Hose	dee hooh-se
address	die Adresse	dee ah-dres-e

Adjectives

Adjectives are used to describe or characterize things or individuals. They are used to make the meanings of sentences clearer or more exact. In general, German adjectives precede the word they modify, and adjectives that come after the noun are not declined. However, adjectives can come before or after the noun while in English they come only before the noun.

The type of ending depends on several factors, including **gender** (der, die, das) and the **noun case** (nominative, accusative, and dative).

"der **gute** Hund" (the good dog), "das **große** Haus" (the big house/building), "die **schöne** Frau" (the pretty woman).

What to consider when learning German adjectives:

German adjectives with a definite article have the endings –**e** or **-en.**

With definite articles the -e is used in the Nominative (singular) case and also in all singular forms where the article "appears" like the Nominative.

So, when does a definite article *appears* like the nominative article? In the Accusative for feminine (die) and neuter (das) are forms where the articles don't change. They always remain "die" or "das". In contrast the masculine "der" changes to a "den" in Accusative.

But in all other situations the definite articles change and require the ending: -en. Additionally, the - en is automatically used in all plural forms.

If it's the Nominative (singular) case or looks like the Nominative then it's an -e. In all other cases an -en.

Examples:
Der alte Mann schaut auf das Meer. - *The old man looks at the sea.*

This is a Nominative form, hence the -e.

Die Frau kauft das elegant**e** Kleid. - The woman buys the elegant dress.

The last example sentence is an Accusative form (das) where the Nominative and Accusative "look" identical, hence the -e.

Kennst du **den** frech**en** Jungen? - Do you know the nasty boy?
"den" is not the Nominative, therefore the -en.
Ich spreche mit der nett**en** Lehrerin. - I am talking with the nice (female) teacher.

The feminine form "die" has changed to "der", therefore it is not identical with the Nominative and is changed into -en.

Telling Time and Date

Germans l have a strong tendency to number everything for some reason, which means numbers play a significant role not only in the language but in everyday life.

Fortunately, German numbers cognate of their English equivalents. German also has both ordinal and cardinal numbers just as English does.

Expressing the Date in German

Germans express the date in the long or short format. In both formats, the day is written before the month and before the year. In addition, the day, month and year are separated by a period or long marks instead of the slash marks usually see in English dates. The day is also expressed as an ordinal number.

The long format:

German		English
der 10.	Juni 2016	the tenth of July 2016

The short format:

German		English
der 08.	04. 2016	04/08/2016

German - English

das/ im Morgengrauen - dawn

der/ am Morgen - morning

der/ am Vormittag - late morning

der/ am Mittag - noon

der/ am Nachmittag - afternoon

der/ am Abend - evening

die/ in der Nacht - night

Telling the Year in German

There are two ways to tell the year in German. For the years before the year 2000, in 1866 for instance, the year is written as achtzehnhundertsechsundsechzig - literally, eighteen hundered sixtysix

For the year 2000 onward, the year is expressed like a regular number. For example, the year 2017 is zweitausendsiebzehn - two thousand seventeen

Cardinal and Ordinal Numbers

In this chapter, you will learn about cardinal numbers, ordinal numbers and fractions.

German numbers, starting from zero to twenty are so- called "unique numbers", that you need to learn independently.

From twenty to ninety-nine the numbers are "dated backwards" (compared to numbers in English). Note that German numbers before number one million are written as one word.

Cardinal and Ordinal Numbers

0 - Null
1 - Eins
2 - Zwei
3 - Drei
4 - vier
5 - Fünf
6 - Sechs
7 - Sieben
8 - Acht
9 - Neun
10 - Zehn
11 - Elf
12 - Zwölf
13 - Dreizehn
14 - Vierzehn
15 - Fünfzehn
16 - Sechzehn
17 - Siebzehn
18 - Achtzehn
19 - Neunzehn
20 - Zwanzig
21 - Einundzwanzig
22 - Zweiundzwanzig
23 - Dreiundzwanzig
24 - vierundzwanzig
25 - Fünfundzwanzig
26 - Sechsundzwanzig

27 - Siebenundzwanzig
28 - Achtundzwanzig
29 - Neunundzwanzig
30 - Dreissig
40 - Vierzig
50 - Fünfzig
60 - Sechzig
70 - Siebzig
80 - Achtzig
90 - Neunzig
100 - Hundert
1000 - Tausend
2000 - Zweitausend
3000 - Dreitausend
4000 - Viertausend
5000 - Fünftausend
10.000 - Zehntausend
100.000 - Hunderttausend
1.000.000 - eine Million
1.000.000.000 - eine Milliarde

Ordinal Numbers

Ordinal numbers are used to indicate and designate placements and rankings of placement. Ordinal numbers are basically adjectives just like regular other German adjectives, actually many of them look familiar with many English adjectives. However, they must change their forms to match the noun or pronoun they modify.

In most cases, ordinal numbers are formed by adding a suffix to the cardinal number. But numbers from one to nineteen need to add the suffix –te while numbers twenty and up get -ste.

The exceptions are:
first (erste), third (dritte), seventh (siebte), and eight (achte).

The -e ending on each ordinal number is in fact an adjective ending. The ending may change based on the case where it appears and, on the gender, and number of the noun it modifies. Possible suffixes are: -e, - en, -er, -es, and less commonly –em.

German Ordinal Numbers

1. erstens – 1st first
2. zweitens – 2nd second
3. drittens – 3rd third
4. viertens – 4th fourth
5. fünftens – 5th fifth
6. sechstens – 6th sixth
7. siebtens / siebentens – 7th seventh
8. achtens – 8th eighth
9. neuntens – 9th ninth
10. zehntens – 10th tenth
11. elftens – 11th eleventh
12. zwölftens – 12th twelfth
13. dreizehntens – 13th thirteenth
14. vierzehntens – 14th fourteenth
15. fünfzehntens – 15th fifteenth
16. sechzehntens – 16th sixteenth
17. siebzehntens – 17th seventeenth
18. achtzehntens – 18th eighteenth
19. neunzehntens – 19th nineteenth
20. zwanzigstens – 20th twentieth
21. einundzwanzigstens – 21st twenty-first
22. zweiundzwanzigstens – 22nd twenty-second
23. dreiundzwanzigstens – 23rd twenty-third
24. vierundzwanzigstens – 24th twenty-fourth
25. fünfundzwanzigstens – 25th twenty-fifth
26. sechstundzwanzigstens – 26th twenty-sixth
27. siebenundzwanzigstens – 27th twenty-seventh
28. achtundzwanzigstens – 28th twenty-eighth
29. neunundzwanzigstens – 29th twenty-ninth
30. dreizigstens – 30th thirtieth
31. einunddreizigstens – 31st thirty-first

40. vierzigstens – 40th fourtieth
42. zweiundvierzigstens – 42nd forty-second
50. fünfzigstens – 50th fiftieth
53. dreiundfünfzigstens – 53rd fifty-third
60. sechzigstens – 60th sixtieth
64. vierundsechzistens – 64th sixty-fourth
70. siebzigstens – 70th seventieth
75. fünfundsiebzigstens – 75th seventy-fifth
80. achtzigstens – 80th eightieth
86. sechsundachzigstens – 86th eighty-sixth
90. neunzigstens – 90th ninetieth
97. siebenundneunzigstens – 97th ninety-seventh
100. hundertstens – 100th hundredth

Fractions

German use Fractions to express partial quantities. To write fractions in German, you will use a cardinal number as a numerator and the stem of the ordinal number the "-el" ending as the denominator. German fractions are formed by adding the suffix -"tel" to the ordinal numbers.

Most forms are invariable, except for "halb" (half), which is inflected like most adjectives to correspond with the noun it modifies.

.

Capitalization and Punctuation

All nouns are capitalized in German, no matter where they appear in a sentence.

The formal "you"(***Sie***) is always capitalized. This also applies to the related forms *Ihnen* and *Ihr*.

Unlike the English "I", the first person singular, the pronoun ***ich*** **is not capitalized,** unless *Ich* begins a sentence. Adjectives describing people, nationality, ethnicity and religion are not capitalized in German.

Typically the format for German quotation marks is „___“ (rather than “___”)

Unlike in English, a comma can link two independent clauses in German.

Take note: It used to be until recently that the ***du*** and its related forms (***dich/dir/euch***) used to be capitalized, just like ***Sie***, and some people (the elderly) still capitalize them, especially in correspondence, **nowadays *du* is written in lowercase.**

Articles and the Four German Noun Cases

In German we have three main articles:

der (masculine), **die** (feminine) and **das** (neuter).

For example:

der Mann (the man)

die Frau (the woman)

das Tier (the animal)

German articles change depending on

the **gender** (masculine, feminine, neuter)

the **number** (singular or plural)

the **case** (nominative, genitive, dative, and accusative)

The different forms can be: **der**, **die**, **das**, **des**, **dem** and **den** depending on gender, number and case.

The best method to get familiar to the articles is by memorizing vocabulary and listening a lot to the German language.

Always try to remember the main articles for **der**, **die** and **das**.

There are several rules and guidelines determining the articles of some categories of nouns. But beware exceptions.

Our tip:
Don't try to understand the usage too much. There are more exceptions than rules. Just treat the article as an integrated part of the noun. Example: door == die Tür. The "die" has no explicit meaning and the gender "female" doesn't make any sense for a door. It's just part of the word.

Rules for Article **'der'**
The following nouns have the article **der**:

- Nouns for masculine persons and functions or professions: der Schaffner, der Vater, der Pilot
- Names of seasons (die Jahreszeiten): der Frühling, der Sommer, der Herbst, der Winter;
- Names of months: der August, der Januar etc.
- Names of days of the week der Montag, der Dienstag etc.
- Names of compass directions: der Westen, der Nordwest(en), der Süd(en) etc

Rules for Article 'die'

The following nouns have the article **die**:

• Nouns for feminine persons, animals, functions/professions: die *Mutter*, *die Friseuse*

• Names of motorcycle brands: die *Harley*, die *BMW*, die *Yamaha, die Honda*

Furthermore, nouns with the suffixes below have the article **die**:

– **falt**: *Vielfalt*;
– **heit**: *Freiheit, Gemeinheit, Sicherheit*;
keit: *Möglichkeit, Helligkeit Schnelligkeit;*
– **schaft**: *Freundschaft, Kameradschaft, Kundschaft, Mannschaft*
– **t** (nouns derived from verbs): *Fahrt, Tat;*
– **ung**: *Leitung, Verfehlung, Zeitung*

Rules for Article 'das'

- The following nouns have the article **das**:
- Diminutives (–**chen, –lein**):
- *Kaninchen, Frauchen, Fräulein;*
- Nouns, derived from infinitives: *Essen,*
- *Spielen Schreiben;*
- Nouns derived from adjectives: *Liebe, Gute,*
- *Böse*
- Names of colors: *Rot, Gelb, Blau*

Note: German sentences often start with the word **das**. This has nothing to do with the article **das**

In German some obvious feminine nouns, such as *das Mädchen, das Fraulein*, still need the neutral articles **das**

Independent from the article der, die or das, the plural is always **die**

Nouns and Noun Cases

German nouns are easily identifiable because they all begin with a capital letter regardless of their position in a sentence.

A noun case is generally indicated by the article that comes before it. Therefore, there are four forms of definite and indefinite articles to identify and modify each case.

In German, nouns can have four cases: Nominative, Accusative, Dative and Genitive.

The Nominative Case

A noun is in the nominative case when a subject or a predicate in a sentence. The following are the definitive and indefinitive articles that modify nouns in the nominative case:

Subject	Definitive	Indefinitive
Masculine	der	ein
Feminine	die	eine
Neuter	das	ein
Plural	die	

The Accusative Case

The accusative is also known as the objective case in English. A German noun can be a direct object of the proposition in the accusative case. Here are the forms of definitive and indefinitive articles tha mark nouns in the accusative case:

Subject	Definitive	Indefinite (a or an)
Masculine	den	einen
Feminine	die	Eine
Neuter	das	Ein
Plural	die	

Take note that only the masculine forms of definite and indefinite articles are declined in the accusative case. For the feminine and neuter gender, you need to use the same articles you normally use in the nominative case.

Nouns as direct object

A noun functioning as a direct object receives the action performed by the subject or shows the effect of the action.

Er spielt das Klavier - *He plays the piano*

Der Mann ißt das Brot - *The man eats the bread*

Das Kind ißt den Fisch - *The child eats the fish*

Nouns as object of accusative prepositions

The following prepositions require nouns as objects in the accusative case:

durch - *through*
fur - *for*
ohne - *without*
um - *at, around*
bis - *until*
wider - *against*
pro - *per*

Das Kind schlief bis Mittag
The child slept until noon

Die Tochter ist gegen die Mutter
The daughter is against the mother

Ich gehe nicht ohne meine Tochter
I don't go without my daughter

Expressions of Time and Distance

Expressions of specific time and distance take the accusative case if they don't follow prepositions:

Er schlief eine Woche im Bahnhof
He slept one week in the train station.

Der Flughafen liegt einen Kilometer von der Garage
The airport is one kilometer from the garage

The Dative Case

The dative case is equivalent to the indirect object in English. German nouns in the dative case perform several functions aside from being an indirect object. In the dative case, the noun, the modifiers and other words connected to it are declined in all genders and numbers. Here are the forms of modifiers in the dative case

Masculine	Dem	einem	keinem	meinem
Feminine	Der	einer	keiner	meiner
Neuter	dem	einem	keinem	meinem
Plural	dem	-	keinen	meinem

Nouns as indirect Object

An indirect Object tells for whom an action is being done.
Klaus geht mit seiner Mutter einkaufen

Klaus goes shopping with his mother

Er gibt meinem Hund einen Knochen
He gives my dog a bone.

Nouns as object of a dative verb or dative construction. Some adjectives, verbs, and idiomatic expressions require a dative object. Here are some verbs that need a dative object, but will never take an accusative object.

to thank
antworten
to trust
vertrauen
to believe
glauben
to occur to
einfallen
to follow
folgen
to be sorrow
leid tun
to be missing
fehlen
to happen
passieren
to damage
schaden
to forgive
verzeihen
to taste
schmecken

Examples:
I thank him
He's missing something
Something can happen to her
I forgive him
He likes (taste) it I believe her

to whom? – zu wem?

Ich danke ihm

Es fehlt ihm was

Es kann ihr was passieren

Ich vergebe ihm

Es schmeckt ihm

Ich glaube ihr

The best way to recognize a dative case is to memorize certain prepositions that always require a dative:

from, out of	aus
except for	ausser
with at	bei
opposite, in relation to	gegenüber
to, according to, after	nach
since, for ¨time period	seit
by, from	von
to	zu

Nouns that function as a dative object and of two-way proposition either indicate a location or form an idiomatic expression.

There are propositions which are called "**two way prepositions**" because you can use them in both accusative and dative case.

Here are the "two way prepositions":

across, about	über
in front of	vor
in, into	in
behind	hinter
to,toward	an
beside	neben
to, onto, toward	auf
under	auf
between	zwischen

The woman lies under the couch.
Die Frau liegt unter dem Sofa.

He is waiting in front of the house.
Er wartet vor dem Haus.

The Genitive Case

The genitive case indicates a relationship or possession. You can easily find the genitive by asking "whose" (wessen). In addition, you can use it as an object of genitive preposition, genitive verb, and genitive construction. This case is also useful in expressing indefinite time. The genitive is defined by specific endings in the articles (des/der), pronouns and adjectives.

To indicate relationship or possessions

In German, any form of possession or relationship is expressed with use of genitive case. This is the equivalent of using the English apostrophe mark and / or "s" or the use of preposition "of" - to indicate possession. For example, in English, you can either say "Tim's books" or "the books of Tim" to express that the books belong to Tim.

The genitive construction usually follow the noun, and it modifies except in cases when you need to use the proper noun to indicate genitive possession. In such cases, you will just add an "s" to the proper name. If Genitive ends in an "s" you will add an apostrophe at the end.

Examples:

Tims' Bruder hat ein Auto gekauft.
Micheal's brother has bought a car.
Sofias' Katze ist krank.
Sofia's cat is sick.

The Genitive case is more commonly used in written German language. In spoken German, however, genitives denoting possessions and relationships are usually supplanted by the pattern "von - plus dative case".

An object of a genitive preposition takes the genitive case in standard German.

Examples:
because of
wegen
within
innerhalb
outside of
ausserhalb
on the basis of
aufgrund
according to
laut
in place of
anstelle

Usage:

Sie kann heute nicht arbeiten wegen ihrer Krankheit

Some adjectives, verbs and idiomatic phrases with genitive

Object:

to make use of
bedienen
to think of
gedenken
to make certain of
sich vergewissern
to be in need of
bedarf

Usage:

Er vergewissert sich, dass er gesund ist.

The following adjectives and idioms require Genitive object:

certain
sicher
suspicious
verdächtigt
guilty
schuldig
innocent
unschuldig
conscious
bewusst

Article Genders, Definite and Indefinite Articles

Definite Article

The definite article is used to talk about a specific subject which is certain or known. It is the equivalent of the English definite article "the". In German, the definite article is declined to reflect the noun's cases, but all forms still mean "the".

Gender	Nominativ	Accusativ	Dativ	Genetiv
Singular				
Masculine	der	den	dem	des
Feminine	die	die	der	der
Neuter	das	das	dem	des
Plural	die	die	den	der

The indefinite article "**ein**"

The indefinite article "ein" and it's other forms translate to the English indefinite articles "a"
or "an" and are only used before singular nouns. Here are the forms of the indefinite article "ein" in different cases:

Gender	Nominativ	Accusativ	Dativ	Genetiv
Singular				
Masculine	ein	einen	einem	eines
Feminine	eine	eine	einer	einer
Neuter	ein	ein	einem	eines

The indefinite article "**kein**"

"Kein" is a negative article, which means "no" or "not". You can use it before both singular and plural nouns.

Gender	Nominativ	Accusativ	Dativ	Gender
Singular				
Masculine	kein	keinen	keinem	keines
Feminine	keine	keine	keiner	keiner
Neuter	kein	kein	keinem	keines
Plural	keine	keine	keinem	keiner

Gender of Nouns

A german noun can be feminine, masculine or neutral. Gender is indicated by an article that appears with the noun.

Feminine Nouns

Female nouns are designated to indicate female persons and female animals:
die Mutter - *the mother*
die Kuh - *the cow*

die Ratte - *the rat*
die Tante - *the aunt*

Nouns ending in -ung, -ei, -keit, -schaft, -tat, - heit, -nis are feminine.

Examples:
die Eitelkeit - *vanity*
die Wirtschaft - *economy*
die Gesundheit - *health*
die Zeitung - *newspaper*
die Erkenntnis - *knowledge*
die Wissenschaft - *science*

Most nouns ending in -e are feminine:
die Reise - *trip / journey*
die Kirche - *church*
die Strasse - *street*

die Leute - people
die Gardine - *curtain*

Masculine Nouns

Nouns that designate male persons and animals:
der Vater - *father*
der Man man
der Stuhl - *chair*
der Computer- *computer*
der Fisch - *fish*

Seasons, days, weeks and month are also masculine nouns:
der Herbst
autumn
der Freitag
Fridays
der Feiertag
holiday

Nouns ending -ich, -ling, -us, -or, -er, -ant are masculine

der Zirkus
circus
der Lieferant
supplier
der Schlachter
butcher
der Mentor
mentor
der Soldat
soldier

Neuter nouns
the following are classified as neutral nouns Humans and animal babies:

das Baby
das Kind
das Kalb

Nouns formed from verb infinitives

das Einkaufen shopping
schlafen *sleep*
das Essen *food*
das Leben *life*

Diminutives

with **-chen** and **-lein**

are neuter nouns:

das Mädchen, das Fräulein, das Männlein

All alphabet letters are neuter nouns.

Gender Peculiarities

Some German nouns which are spelled the same have totally different meanings and therefore are not necessarily neuter nouns

der See *lake*
die See *ocean*
das Gehalt *salary*
der Gehalt *contents* (chem.)
die Leiter *ladder*
der Leiter *leader*

Compound Nouns and their Gender

The German language is famous for its long nouns. These are the so called compound nouns, which refer to nouns formed by combining two or more words. Compound nouns can be combination of nouns, adverbs, adjectives, prepositions, and verb, stems, but must always have a noun as the last element. The German language include many inventions of compound nouns, hence, you can find many of them.

Examples:

die Zeit+frei	die Freizeit	free time
das Haus+der Schuh	der Hausschuh	slippers
schnell + der Zug	der Schnellzug	fast train
die Haupt+die Stadt	die Hauptstadt	capitol

Pluralizing Nouns

Plural nouns are indicated by the definite article "die" for all genders. There are exceptions, but German nouns take the following endings to express the plural.

Endings with -en Examples:

Singular	Plural	Meaning
die Lehrerin	Die Leherrinnen	female teachers
die Datei	die Dateien	files
die Fabrik	die Fabriken	factories

Most masculine and feminine nouns ending in -e form, but in some rare cases, neuter nouns with -e endings take the -n ending in the plural

Examples:

die Lampe	die Lampen	lamp
die Blume	die Blumen	flowers
das Auge	die Augen	eyes

-e or an umlaut in the stem + -e

Almost 90% of masculine nouns, about 25% of feminine nouns and around 75% of neuter nouns form the *Plural* with the patterns -e Feminine nouns that form their *Plural* with-e always take an umlaut.

Some neuter nouns form the *Plural* with -er or an umlaut in the sem -er

Examples:

das Kind	die Kinder	children
das Gesicht	die Gesichter	faces
das Bild	die Bilder	images

Adjective Nouns

Adjective nouns are those nouns which are formed from adjectives or participles, functioning as adjectives. Some are useful in determining masculine or feminine nouns. They are declined like adjectives

Examples:

Adjective	Adjectival Nouns	Adjective	Noun
bekannt	der/die Bekannte	known	acquaintance
blind	der/die Blinde	blind	blind person
fremd	der Fremde/die Fremde	foreign	foreigners

<u>Neuter adjectival nouns</u> are used to refer to concepts or ideas.

Examples:

Adjective	Adjectival Noun	Adjective	Noun
gut	das Gute	good	the good thing
ganz	das Ganze	whole	the whole thing
neu	das Neue	new	the new

Infinite Nouns

A verb in its infinitive form works as a noun by capitalizing the initial letter. All infinitive nouns are neuter and generally correspond to the English gerund form.

Examples:

German infinitive	Meaning	Infinitive Noun	Meaning
trinken	to drink	das Trinken	drinking
lesen	to read	das Lesen	reading
einkaufen	to shop	das Einkaufen	shopping

Pronouns

Pronouns take the place of nouns. In general, German pronouns agree with the case, number and gender of the noun they replace. Pronouns are categorized as personal, possessive, reflective, relative, demonstrative, indefinite and interrogative.

Personal Pronouns

Both German and English pronouns have different forms to indicate number, gender and case. German, however, has two forms of pronouns to express "you" - the informal and formal. In addition, the informal " you" has a separate form to distinguish the plural.

The singular informal form of "**you**" is "**du**", and its plural form is "ihr". It addresses children and people who are on familiar with the speaker.

The formal form of "**you**” ist "**Sie**" in both plural and singular. It uses the same conjugation patterns as used in third person, it always begins with a capital letter. It usually addresses older people, superiors, and new acquaintances.

The German pronoun for **they** is "**sie**", which is written in lower case letters, unless it's used to start a new sentence.

Personal pronouns are commonly used in the nominative case.

Here are the plural and singular forms of personal pronouns in the nominative, accusative, dative and genitive cases.

Interrogative Pronouns

German interrogative pronouns are question words that usually begin with "w". Many interrogative pronouns have direct English translation.

Examples:

Was? - What?

Warum? - Why?

Wie? - How?

Wann? - When?

The German words for "who" and "where", however, deviate from their English equivalent pronoun.

The question word "who" is declined in all cases:

Case	Pronoun	Meaning
Nom.:	wer?	who?
Acc.:	wen?	whom?
Dat.:	wem?	to whom?
Gen.:	wessen?	whose?

Reflexive Pronouns

Reflexive pronouns are frequently used in German. They are used as direct or indirect objects in sentences with a reflexive verbs, and are only used in the dative or accusative case. They are more commonly used in German than in English because there are more reflexive verbs in German.

Verbs and Moods

In general, German verbs are conjugated to reflect the mood, tense, person, gender and number.

Verb moods:

The mood of a verb indicates the attitude or perception of the speaker towards what is being expressed in a sentence.

The German language has four verb moods. The indicative, subjunctive 1, subjunctive 2 and the imperative mood.

The indicative Mood

Subjunctive (Konjunktive) 1

Subjunctive (Konjunktive) 2

The Imperative Mood

German Verb Types and Irregulars

German verbs end in -n or -en in the infinitive form and may be grouped into the following categories:

Auxiliary verbs
Modal verbs
Regular verbs
Irregular verbs
Mixed verbs

Auxiliary verbs

Modal verbs have the following forms in the present tense tablet

The modal verb takes the second position while the main verb is place at the end of the sentence

Examples:

Regular verbs

Regular verbs or weak verbs follow a predictable pattern of conjugation and never change their stem when conjugated. To form the different tenses, you simply use the present infinitive stem and add the endings under each mood, tense, and person.

The present indicative tense has the following endings

(Subject) - Endings

ich - e

du - st

er/sie/es - t

wir - en

ihr - t

sie/Sie - en

For verb stems ending in-t, -d, -m, or -n, the du form, er/sie/es forms, and ihr form add - e before the regular endings to ease pronunciation.

To conjugate a verb you will have the following forms of regular verbs and irregular verbs

Irregular Verbs

Irregular verbs or strong verbs change their stem to indicate verb tenses. Stem changes are generally unpredictable, and you need to learn them individually. In addition, irregular verbs do not always change their stem to convey every tense. All German irregular verbs, however, add -en to form the past participle.

To...(English)	Infinitive Form	Present
Tense		
move	bewegen	bewegt
tie	binden	bindet
find	finden	findet

Mixed Verbs

Mixed verbs take specific characteristics from both regular and irregular verbs they add the suffix -e to form the past participle, and simple past. Like irregular verbs they change their stem when conjugated.

denken - dachte - (hat) gedacht
think - thought - thought

German Tenses and Verb Tenses

Active and Passive Voice

In the passive voice, the subject of the sentence is the receiver of object of the verb's action. To construct sentences in the passive voice, you will use the conjugated form of werden + the past participle of the main verb. The subject is usually not expressed in passive sentences but may be indicated with the use of von + dative noun case. This is the equivalent of the expression *done by...* in English.

Die Filme werden jeden Tag gesehen.

The movies are seen every day

The Verbs: *sein* and *haben*

Sein -to be-, haben -to have-, and werden -to become- are the most common verbs in German. They are irregular verbs that function as **auxiliary verbs** to form compound verb tenses.

Sein (to be)

The verb sein has irregular forms like its English counterpart.

	Present	Past Perfect
Ich	bin (I am)	war (I was)
du	bist (you are)	warst (you were)
er/sie/es	ist (he/she/it)	war (he/she/it was)
wir	sind (we are)	waren (we were)
ihr	seid (you are)	wart (you were)
sie/Sie	sind (they/you are)	waren (they/you were

The verbs "sein" und "haben" are both used in constructing the perfect sense. In German perfect tense is used in most situations.

Ich bin nach Frankreich gereist

I have traveled to France

Haben (to have)

The verb haben has the following conjugation in the present tense:

ich	habe	(I have)
du	hast	(you have)
er/sie/es	hat	(has)
wir	haben	(we have)
ihr	habt	(you have)
sie/Sie	haben	(they have)

Our Tip:

When to use "sein" or "haben" as auxiliary verb: Sein is used with the verbs "werden", "sein", "bleiben", and "passieren". In all other cases, the auxiliary verb "haben" is used.

Verb Tenses

Each German verb tense has a direct English counterpart. Look at the two simple tenses. These tenses are called "simple" because they consist of only one verb. They happen to be rather "simple" to learn as well.

Simple present tense

The present tense is formed by removing the -en ending from a verb, and replacing it with the prescribed ending, depending on the subject of the verb (the noun or pronoun that is doing the verb). This process is known as conjugation. For example, the verb machen (to do or to make) is conjugated like this:

machen (to do/to make): present tense

ich	mache	/ wir	machen
du	machst	/ ihr	macht
sg. noun/pronoun	macht/	pl. noun/pronoun	machen

In the chart you see the nouns, changings and endings you'll want to memorize.

Some verbs require a vowel change for the "du" form and the singular-noun/pronoun-forms. After some practice you'll start to recognize these the more you get familiar with the language.

German has only one present tense form of verbs. This is a very direct form as it catches all tenses for expressing things that are happening right now. In English, the present tense is divided into three forms: simple present tense - I do; the present continuous - I am doing; and the present perfect continuous - I have been doing

Simple Past Tense / Past Tense

Most verbs in the simple past tense are formed in a similar manner to the simple present tense. You still remove the *-en* from the verb, only you add a different set of conjugational endings.

Most of the conjugations use the same ending as the present with a -t added to the beginning of the ending, but with one exception. Can you tell which is it?

The conjugational paradigm for most verbs in the simple past tense is formed like this:

machen (to do/to make): simple past tense

ich	*machte*	*wir*	*machten*
du	*machtest*	*ihr*	*machtet*
sg. noun/pronoun	*machte*	l. noun/pronoun	*machten*

Have you seen the difference? The ending for verbs conjugated for singular nouns but pronouns take a *-te* ending, just like the *ich*-form. You might notice that this *-te* is similar to the -ed ending in English. But just like English, there are some verbs that have a different form in the simple past tense.

Below is an example of a strong verb conjugated in the simple past tense:

schwimmen (to swim): simple past tense

ich	*schwamm*	*wir*	*schwammen*
du	*schwammt*	*ihr*	*schwammt*
sg.	*schwamm*	pl.	*schwamm*

Present Perfect / Conversational Past

The present perfect tense is our first compound tense, meaning we use more than one verb to form these tenses. The present perfect tense contains two verb elements, an auxiliary (or helping) verb and the past participle of a verb. We have the same elements in our present perfect tense in English: I have walked, Has he done it?, We have become. Just like in English, we only have to conjugate the helping verb, *haben*. The past participle stays the same regardless of the subject.

Here's *machen* in its present perfect tense:

machen (to do/to make): present perfect tense

ich	*habe gemacht*	*wir*	*haben gemacht*
du	*hast gemacht*	*ihr*	*habt gemacht*
sg. noun/pronoun	*hat gemacht*	pl. noun/pronoun	*haben gemacht*

You only have to change the ending on the past participle if the verb is weak (takes no vowel change in the simple past). Strong verbs (those whose vowels change in the simple past) keep their -*en* on the past participle. Thus the past participle of *fahren* is *gefahren*. Some strong verbs also have a vowel change in their past participles. These too have to be memorized Past perfect.

The Past Perfect

The last of the past tenses is the past perfect. This one is very similar to the present perfect. It's formed with a helping verb and a past participle, where only the helping verb *sein* or *haben* will be in its simple past form, which is *waren* or *hatten*. The past participle is the same as in the present perfect.

Past Perfect:

machen **- to make**

ich	*hatte gemacht*	*wir*	*hatten gemacht*
du	*hattest gemacht*	*ihr*	*hattet gemacht*
sg. noun/pronoun	*hatte gemacht*	pl. noun/pronoun	*hatten gemacht*

Future Tense

The future tense is another one of our compound tenses with two verbs. The first of these is the verb *werden*, the future marker. Secondly, we use the normal infinitive of a verb at the end of our clause. This is akin to English's future construction with will, as in, "He will go with them." In German this would be, *Er wird mit ihnen gehen. Werden* is the auxiliary verb, thus the only conjugated verb in the future tense.

Future tense

machen

to make

ich	*werde machen*	*wir*	*werden machen*
du	*wirst machen*	*ihr*	*werdet machen*
sg.	*wird machen*	pl.	*werden*

Although the future can mostly be expressed using the present tense in German if it can be understood by context, we use the future with *werden* in situations where it's not so obvious Future perfect tense

Our last tense is also a compound tense, but it's the only one that is made up of three verbs instead of two, which makes it a bit trickier. We'll be using forms that we've already learned from our other tenses, namely the future marker *werden*, the perfect auxiliaries *sein* or *haben*, and the past participle, the same three verb forms we need to make the future perfect tense in English.

Since we can only have one conjugated verb per clause, that means the other verbs, *sein* or *haben* (as well as the past participle) will be left unconjugated.

Let's have a look at a *machen* in the future perfect tense:

Future Perfect Tense

***machen* to make**

ich	*werde gemacht haben*	*wir*	*werden gemacht haben*
du	*wirst gemacht haben*	*ihr*	*werdet gemacht haben*
sg. noun/pronoun	*wird gemacht haben*	pl. noun/pronoun	*werden gemacht haben*

Of course if you're working with a verb that normally requires the use of *sein* as its helping verb, just trade out *haben* for *sein*.**Reflexive Verbs**

Reflexive verbs are much more used in German as they are in English, and they occur in two cases: The accusative and dative case. Most often they are used to describe personal hygiene body care, and personal interactions. They are generally placed after the verb.

Examples:

Er rasiert sich *He's shaving himself*

Ich ziehe mich um. *I am dressing myself*

Sie duscht sich *She is taking a shower*

Reflexive verbs are preceded by the reflexive pronoun "sich" when listed as an infinitive in a standard dictionary.

<u>Most common reflexive verbs:</u>

to be angry sich ärgern

to hurry sich beeilen

to drink too much sich besaufen

to take a bath sich baden

to clean myself sich waschen

to shower sich duschen

to remember sich erinnern

o turn around sich umdrehen

to dress sich ankleiden

to sit down sich setzen

to meet sich treffen

to fall in love sich verlieben

Adjectives

Adjectives are words that describe or modify nouns or pronouns. In general,, German adjectives precede the word they modify.

"der **gute** Mann" (the good man), "das **große** Haus" (the big house/building), "die **schöne** Dame" (the pretty lady).

Unlike English adjectives, German adjectives in front of a noun ending (**-e** in the examples above). The type of ending depends on several factors, including **gender** (der, die, das) and **case** (nominative, accusative, and dative).

What to consider when learning German adjectives:

German adjectives with a definite article only ever have the endings -e or -en.

With definite articles the -e is used in the Nominative (singular) and in all singular forms where the article "looks" like the Nominative. To clarify: When does a definite article *look* like a nominative article? In the Accusative for feminine (die) and neuter (das) - forms where the articles don't change. They remain "die" or "das". (In contrast the masculine "der" changes to a "den" in the Accusative.) But in all other instances the definite articles change and require the adjective ending -en. And yes, the - en is also automatically used in all plural forms. So: If it's the Nominative (singular) or looks like it, it's an -e. In all other cases an -en.

Examples:

Der alte Mann schaut auf das Meer. (The old man looks at the sea.)

This is a Nominative form, hence the -e.

Die Frau kauft das elegant**e** Kleid. (The woman buys the elegant dress.)

This is an Accusative form (das) where the Nominative and Accusative "look" identical, hence the -e.

Kennst du den frech**en** Jungen? (Do you know the nasty boy?)

"den" doesn't look like the Nominative, therefore the -en

Ich spreche mit der nett**en** Lehrerin. (I am talking with the nice [female] teacher.)

The feminine form “die” has changed to a “der”, therefore it is not identical with the Nominative and is -en.

Chevrolet baut die besten Autos. (Chevrolet builds the best cars.)

Learn How to Decline the Easy Way

Declension of Adjectives

So-called attributive adjectives are declined in different ways, depending on the case, and their manner of delension is always dependent on the type of modifiers or determiners.

Strong Declension

Strong declension is required when the modifiers of articles are used to have endings that do not clearly indicate the case, a number or gender of the word being modified.

Strong declension is used in the following situations:

1. No article is used

2. When the adjective appears after a number or number-adjective with no ending.

3. When the adjective comes after a pronoun other than "mir", "dir" and "ihm"

The adjective comes after "mehr" (more), or "etwas" (something/some)
The adjective is always preceded by "ein paar" (a couple, a few, "ein wenig", "ein bisschen" (a few, a little), "mehrere"(some/a couple of),"folgende" (the following).

Weak Declension

Weak declension is used when determiners have endings which clearly express the case, gender and number of the noun being modified.

Adjectives that require weak declension may only take the "e" or "en" ending.

The following situations warrant the use of weak adjective declension:

1. When the adjective comes after a definite article.

2. When it follows the pronoun "dieser" (this), "jener"(that), or "jeglich(e)" (any)

3. When the adjective appears after "dir", "mir" and "ihm"

4. When thee adjective is placed after "alle"(all) and/or "beide" (both)

5.When the adjective comes after "welcher/e" (which) and/or "solch, solcher" (such)

.

Weak declension singular

SG.	*Masculinum*	*Feminum*	*Neutrum*
Nominativ	der Wein	die Wurst	das Bier
	der kalte Wein	die kalte Wurst	das kalte Bier
Genitiv	**des** Weines	**der** Wurst	**des** Biers
	des kalten Weines	**der** kalten Wurst	**des** kalten Biers
Dativ	**dem** Wein	**der** Wurst	**dem** Bier
	dem kalten Wein	**der** kalten Wurst	**dem** kalten Bier
Akkusativ	**den** Wein	die Wurst	das Bier
	den kalt**en** Wein	die kalt**e** Wurst	das kalt**e** Bier

Weak decle nsion plural

PL.	*Masculinum*	*Feminum*	*Neutrum*
Nominativ	die kalten Weine	die kalten Würste	die kalten Biere
Genitiv	der kalten Weine	der kalten Würste	der kalten Biere
Dativ	den kalten Weinen	den kalten Würsten	den kalten Bieren
Akkusativ	die kalten Weine	die kalten Würste	die kalten Biere

With indefinite articles for example, all forms of - *kein, mein, dein,* the ending is always: -en, also in cases where you have -en with definite articles.

Indefinite articles (incl. all forms of *kein, mein, dein* -possessive etc) the ending is always -en in exactly the cases where we also have an -en with definite articles.

Mixed Declension

Mixed declension is used when the adjective is placed after so-called possessive determiners which include the infinitive articles "ein" and "kein".

German Possessive Adjectives

In German the use of possessive adjectives is the way to show ownership.

.

German	English
mein	mine
deine	your
sein	his
ihr	her
unser	our
euer	your
ihr	their

With indefinite articles for example, all forms of - *kein, mein, dein,* the ending is always: -en, also in cases where you have -en with definite articles.

Indefinite articles (incl. all forms of *kein, mein, dein* -possessive etc) the ending is always -en in exactly the cases where we also have an -en with definite articles.

.

Adverbs

Adverbs are words which describe the action of a verb, adjectives or other adverbs

Most adjectives can also be used as adverbs without adding a suffix. In fact, when those adjectives are used as adverbs they have no endings at all.

In German, adverbs have been divided into four groups. The groups describe when, how and where things happen, therefore they are called adverbs of time, manner and place.

Locative Adverbs

Locative adverbs can be the answer to the questions: "Where/Where - to/where - and from?"

aufwärts	upwards
außen	outside
da	here/there
dort	there/over there
drinnen	inside
fort	away
hier	here
(bis)hierhin	up to here
hinein	into
hinten	behind
irgendwo	somewhere
links	left (of)
nebenan	near

oberhalb	above
überall	everywhere
unten	below
vorn	in front

Example:

Als wir ankamen, stand unsere Familie schon ganz hinten auf dem Parkplatz

Temporal Adverbs

Temporal adverbs answer the questions "when/how long, how often, until when, since when"

bald	soon
bereits	.already
bisher danach	until now thereafter
davor .einst	beforehand once
endlich	eventually/finally
freitags	Fridays
gestern	yesterday
immer	always
inzwischen	meanwhile

Example:

Gestern war ich mit Freunden auf einem Rockkonzert.

Modal Adverbs

Modal adverbs are the answer to the questions “How/How much?"

anders	different
.äußerst	extremely
beinahe	nearly
bekanntlich	famously
ebenfalls	likewise
fast	almost
folgendermaßen	.as follows
ganz	completely
genauso	exactly like
.genug	enough
gern	gladly

Example:

Ich habe in meinem Leben genug Steuern bezahlt.

Causal Verbs

Anstandshalber - *for decency's sake*

Dadurch - *through that./because of that, that*

Darum - *therefore/because of*

Demnach - *thus/according to that*

Demzufolge - *whereby/accordingly*

Deshalb - therefore

Example:

Unsere Freunde warteten deshalb nicht auf uns

German Idioms

Idiomatic expressions are commonly used expressions by Germans speakers that have a figurative, but quite often not a literal meaning. These expressions define the variety of the local culture, and most languages have them. English has a long list of terms and idioms, and so does German. Sometimes idioms may appear meaningless and vague. But it's important to learn what these expressions mean in order for you to fully understand the richness of German language.

There are German idioms that have a direct English translation. Being able to use these idioms won't be too hard for you. For example, the German phrase **hau ab** which direct translation means "strike down", but the real meaning is "get out of here", or "beat it!"

Another famous one is **Daumen drücken**, when translated, means “pressing your thumb”, which is near to the English idiom: “to cross your fingers”.

There are other German expressions that can take time to understand. For example, the phrase **Was du heute kannst besorgen, das verschiebe nicht auf morgen**, which when taken apart and translated word for word mean *"What you can today don't do it tomorrow"*.

A few other typical German idioms are:

Ich verstehen nur Bahnhof
Literal translation: *I can only understand train station*

Das geht mir auf den Geist
Literal translation: This is going on my host. Means: *This is bothering me.*

Jemanden Honig um den Bart schmieren
Literal translation: To smear honey on someones beard. Means: *To make false compliments.*

Schwein gehabt
Literal translation: Had a pig. Means: *I/you/we/anyone got very lucky*

Dumm wie Toastbrot
Literal translation: Stupid as toasted bread. Means: *Someone is very stupid*

Jemanden durch den Kakao ziehen
Literal translation: To pull someone through chocolate.
Meaning: *Not to take s.o. serious*

PRACTICAL
LEARNING GUIDE
NEW AND ACCELERATED
LEARNING METHODS
ACADEMY DER SPRACHCLUB
Language
Starter
Book

Part 2

Practical Learning Guide

New and Accelerated Learning Methods

Since we are associated with a private language school we had years to observe which teaching and learning methods work and which don't. For many years we already had refined our own system; we just kept it to our daily teaching practices until some of our students convinced us to publish them. Actually, it is more like a guide, and if followed correctly will bring lasting results. If applied in a disciplined fashion, you surely will be able to expand your German in a short time.

Most students of this book are beginners or intermediate level learners, which means they have only limited knowledge of

German, and most likely no idea about the language structure, leave alone any or cultural background of the language and people.

So, let's get started by getting an overview on how to work with the material.

Before you start to learn these "accelerated methods", please go back to the beginning of this book and scroll down until you find the alphabet. Read the pronunciation section and notice the few differences in the German alphabet. Write down those vowels you think are difficult. Let it sink into your head, take notes, and you are basically ready to take the first steps.

The point is, with the help of this step-by-step approach is, you are your own designer of your personal **big "German Plan".**

The following methods should be implemented in the suggested sequence. We will elaborate on them in the next chapter:

1. Surround yourself with German voices, which can be movies, music, and recordings.

2. Then you will try to speak what you have heard.

3. Slowly, by combining the audio experiences with the study material you will get a "German brain" and with exposing yourself into a German environment you will partially adapt the mentality - We explain you more...

4. you will learn German phrases and expressions

5. You will learn not only to pronounce, but to speak German.

6. As a last step you must learn some of the grammar and structures of the language.

Of course, you can elaborate on these methods and add your own ideas. It's important that you follow the methods slowly at your own pace, step-by-step, which means you don't rush to the next step or exercise before not finishing with your current level and task.

Getting Started: Implement the New Methods Step-By-Step

Use the following methods and you will find learning German not only more more enjoyable, but a more engaging and speedy process. You should learn a new language in an enjoyable environment, but at the same time keep your work discipline and follow the steps in sequence.

What we call the "big German plan" is actually a of non-traditional learning methods that can give you a beneficial start and to advance fast to learning the German language.

You will see now an overview of each part of this plan and how you can use it effectively:

Step 1 - Listen to German Voices as much as possible

There is no substitute to expose yourself regularly to the German language to fine-tune your listening skills to the particular way that Germans talk.

There is a wide range of source material online available, for instances YouTube is available anytime for you to listen to and digest. Another good method is to listen to German podcast or recorded short stories for learners. Best are those that contain a lot natural dialogue. By listening to German stories, you can raise the difficulty and complexity whenever you feel ready.

Alternatively, if you don't have internet access, you can tune into German radio stations or satellite TV to get yourself used to hearing conversations.

Step 2 - Start reading phrases, try to memorize vocabulary, and start reading short stories for learners

As mentioned before comprehending the language fast with lasting results is the aim of this plan. It's one thing to be able to pick out words that you already understand, but another to understand what is being said and discussed as a whole.

A very important step to get a better understanding of any discussion and towards better understanding the language in general is simply o memorize vocabulary. You can either use repetition or word association to commit new words to memory. With each new word learnt, another piece of the jigsaw puzzle is put into place. So memorizing vocabulary on a consistent basis is key!

Another valuable additional method is to read short stories aimed at beginners. Books aimed at learners will take particular care to review key vocabulary contained within it and by offering parallel text you will get a complete comprehension of what the story was about.

Step 3 - Get into a German speaking environment

Experience shows, the best way to teach you 'real' conversational German is by putting yourself in a German speaking environment. Whether you do so by studying in a group, travelling, or by joining a 'German only' speaking arena will teach you a great deal about the way Germans express themselves.

Step 4 - Get yourself a "German Mentality"

Additionally, to the 'total immersion' methods of learning is to write down what you think German "is".

Having studied videos, German stories and other German source content, you should try to copy their behavior in certain scenarios.

This is not as difficult as it may sound. Even if you are a beginner, this method can be very helpful when combined with a so-called role play. By trying to talk through an issue or scenario you already have "invented" yourself, you just will highlight "gaps" in your knowledge and ultimately teach yourself new ways of saying things.

Step 5 - Speak whenever possible without worrying

A huge step for any student of German, is the point at which you start to talk and interact with the language. Many of us don’t like the sound of our own voices (especially in a foreign language), but don't worry. By practicing at home on your own or better with a fellow learner, and constantly writing down German expressions, words and phrases, you will increase your confidence in speaking German. Your aim must be to become a "part of the language"

Step 6 - Study grammar and traditional learning material as a last step

All the methods discussed earlier are extremely helpful in helping a learner to master the language, yet it is important to use traditional learning material such as dictionaries, audio, and a German speaking environment to bring everything together. It is your responsibility to seek help and find a holistic approach.

Words, phrases and grammar study, which you will have studied or heard conversationally must be put into context and you must try to comprehend to the language as a whole and study in a pace that keeps you connected to German life, the mentality as well as the language to connect your mind to the German way of thinking. Only then, when you get into the German mindset, into the culture, the environment, the German logic and its consequences, you will be on the right path and the language itself will become a part of you.

This is what you should do additionally:

Expand your vocabulary by reading German short stories

As mentioned earlier, reading short stories is an excellent way to improve your knowledge of the language and to expand your vocabulary. We have included three suitable short stories for beginners, that you should try to read as much as you can even if you don't understand all of it. Each story is followed by a summary and a vocabulary section where you can compare the most important word without using a dictionary

After each story you find an exercise section, where you need to memorize situations and answer the questions to the best of your ability. Exercises are important and should not be skipped.

15 ENTERTAINING
GERMAN
SHORT STORIES
FOR BEGINNERS
INCLUDING AUDIO
ACADEMY DER SPRACHCLUB
Language
Starter
Book

Part 3

15 Entertaining German Short Stories For Beginners + Audio

Short Stories for German Language Students

Here is what you get from this part

In this part you find 15 modern and entertaining German short stories for learners suitable for beginners and intermediate students. Each story is followed by English parallel text in blocks, plot summaries, a key vocabulary section, exercises, and audio, whereby each story comes with its own audio.

The last stories are written for advanced beginners and intermediate students, they are slightly longer, are written in a single block and contain most of the vocabulary of the previous stories. **Each story is also accompanied by audio.**

Learning German through entertaining stories

Reading entertaining short stories to improve your German is an easy way to improve your language skills. This book contains a selection of 20 short stories all prepared specifically for beginners and so-called advanced beginners They come with questions and key-vocabulary. The aim of this book is to teach different topics, words and phrases associated with them in a short period of time

Advance with each story

Each of the short stories for beginners take about 2 minutes to read and average about 100 to 350 words. Important words and phrases relevant to each topic were selected carefully. The vocabulary gets slightly more complex as you advance reading the stories, the last stories contain most of the previously mentioned vocabulary. The stories for intermediate students take about 3-4 minutes to read and average about 300 - 600 words.

The content is intended mainly for elementary to intermediate level learners, but it will be useful for more advanced learners. The short stories have been arranged according to their degree of difficulty.

Follow our tips and how to use the audio

For the absolute language beginner, it might be more beneficial if you listen to the stories first. After reading each story you should review the key-vocabulary section and reread the story once more or repeat reading them until you get a grasp of the story.

Vocabulary will be introduced at a reasonable pace, so you're not overwhelmed with difficult words and much of the vocabulary will be repeated in the exercise section. Some stories are focused on dialogue. These stories contain naturally spoken dialogue, so you can learn conversational German as you read. However, it is more important to finish reading the story without stopping than to understand every word. The simple truth is that you won't get everything your first time around which is completely normal.

Der Einsiedler

The hermit

Timm ist ein **Einsiedler**, sagen die Leute. Aber das ist nur **zum Teil richtig**.
Richtig ist, er lebt abgeschieden im Süden des Bundeslandes Sachsens, nahe der tschechischen **Grenze, außerhalb** eines Dorfes im Erzgebirge.
Ein Einsiedler ist meistens arm an **materiellen Gütern** und so ist es auch bei Tim. Keine elektrische Heizung, und genaugenommen auch keinen Strom. Den kann er sich aber gelegentlich zum Kochen besorgen, denn er hat einen Herd, und draußen vor seinem Haus, hat er einen Generator angeschlossen.

People say, Tim is a hermit. But that's just partly true.
True is, he is living abandoned in the southern state of Saxony, near to the border of the Czech Republic outside of a village in the Erzgebirge mountains. A hermit is mostly poor in material goods and so it is with Tim. No electric radiator and strictly speaking not even electricity. But he can get some for cooking for he has a stove and in front of his house he has linked a generator.

Wasser gibt es reichlich, im hinteren Bereich seine **Behausung** fließt Wasser quasi vom Dach direkt an einer Wand herunter, und verschwindet im Boden. Ansonsten ist er eingerichtet. Ein großes Bett, kleine Schränke für die Nischen, eine selbstgebaute Camping Toilette, Stereoanlage, Farbfernseher, und für seinen

Computer leistet er sich Internet mit **Anschluss**. Zum **Aufladen** seiner kleineren Geräte fährt er mit dem Fahrrad zum Nachbarn. Einmal in der Woche fährt er mit dem Fahrrad ins 10 Kilometer entfernte Dorf, wo er im Supermarkt billig einkauft. Tim hat noch einen **Traum**, er möchte eine moderne Toilette, und noch wichtiger, ein richtiges, geschlossenes Panoramafenster.

There is enough water; in the back area of his dwelling water virtually flows off the roof and along the wall until it disappears in the floor. Otherwise he is well equipped. A big bed, little wardrobes for the alcoves, a handmade camping toilet, a stereo, a color TV set and for his computer he treats himself to internet with a satellite connection. For charging his smaller devices he goes by bike to his distant neighbors.
Once a week he drives with his bicycle to the village which is 10 miles away, where he goes cheaply shopping in the supermarket. Tim has a dream, he likes to have a modern toilet and, even more important, a real, closed panorama window.

Das Problem ist, seine Behausung hat mehrere kleinere Eingänge und nach vorne hin einen riesigen, über fünf Meter breiten Eingang. **Der Eingang** bleibt eigentlich immer offen, denn es passt keine Tür rein, und Plastikfolie hilft nicht immer, wenn es draußen regnet und kalt ist.
Aber **der Blick** aus diesem riesigen Eingang ist fantastisch. Tim lebt umgeben von Bergen und Wald, und von hier aus kann er auf ein weites Tal und auf die **gegenüberliegenden** Bergen blicken. Der Blick inspiriert Tim. Er fühlt sich noch jung und möchte eines Tages Architekt werden. Wenn das nicht funktioniert, dann vielleicht **Schriftsteller**, oder Künstler.

The problem is, his dwelling has several smaller entrances and at the front a huge, over five meters wide entrance. The entrance is actually opened most of the time for there is no door that fits and plastic foil doesn't help, if it's cold and raining outside. But the view out of this enormous entrance is fantastic. Tim lives surrounded by mountains and wood and from here he can look at a wide valley and at the opposite mountains. The view inspires Tim. He feels still young and one day he wants to become an architect. If this doesn't work, maybe he will become a writer or artist.

Ein weiteres Problem ist, es passt keine Tür, kein Fenster in die ungewöhnliche Form des riesigen Eingangs. Freunde haben ihn besucht, aber die Situation erscheint auch ihnen extrem schwierig.
Sie sagen, da Tim in einer **Höhle**, wo vor zehntausend Jahren Bären und Neandertaler lebten, sei es unmöglich dort ein Panoramafenster einbauen zu lassen.

One more problem is that no door and no window are fitting into the unusual form of this huge entrance. Friends have visited him but even for them the situation seemed quite difficult. They say that it's impossible to install a panorama window there, for Tim is living in a cave where ten thousand years ago bears and early humans used to live.

Zusammenfassung

Tim lebt als Einsiedler und träumt davon sich ein großes Panoramafenster einbauen zu lassen. Obwohl er in seiner Behausung gut leben kann, ist es schwierig. Es ist nicht möglich ein Panoramafenster einzubauen, wenn man in einer Höhle lebt.

Vokabeln

der Einsiedler hermit

zum Teil richtig partly true

die Grenze border

außerhalb outside of /out of town

materiellen Gütern material goods / assets

die Behausung dwelling

der Anschluss connection

aufladen charge

der Traum dream

der Eingang entrance

der Blick view

gegenüberliegend opposite

der Schriftsteller writer

die Höhle cave

Beantworte die folgenden Fragen im Auswahlverfahren. Nur eine Antwort je Frage ist richtig

1. Im welchem Bundesland lebt Tim?
a) Er lebt in Hamburg
b) Er lebt im Ausland
c) Er lebt in Berlin
d) Er lebt in Sachsen

2. Was hat Tim vor dem Haus angeschlossen?
a) Einen Generator
b) Einen Herd
c) Eine Waschmaschine
d) Einen Fernseher

3.Was mochte Tim eines Tags beruflich machen?
a) Er möchte Architekt werden
b) Er möchte Koch werden
c) Er hat keine festen Plane
d) Er möchte Lehrer werden

4. Was macht Tim einmal die Woche?
a) Er besucht seine Eltern
b) Er fährt mit dem Fahrrad ins Dorf
c) Er fährt mit dem Bus nach Berlin
d) Er kocht sich warmes Essen

Lösungen
1 d
2 a
3 a
4 b

AUDIO (copy and paste into your browser)

http://bit.ly/2KtscvH

Der Baumarkt
The Homecenter

Lena hatte schon seit Jahren vor, sich eine neue Küche **anzuschaffen**. Das Problem lag darin, dass sie noch bei ihren Eltern wohnte, genau genommen im **Dachgeschoss.**
Dort gab es eine kleine **Kochnische,** ähnlich wie in einem Hotel, ausgestattet mit Mikrowelle und Kaffeemaschine. Lena hatte schon immer gerne in Kochbüchern **gestöbert**, auch hatte sie sich schon hunderte von Koch Rezepten auf Amazon heruntergeladen, und sie war auch eine gute Köchin.

For years, Lena had been planning to acquire a new kitchen. The problem was that she was still living at her parents' home, strictly speaking on the attic. There was a little kitchenette, similar like in an old hotel, equipped with a microwave oven and a coffee machine. Lena had always loved to rummage in cookbooks and had already downloaded hundreds of recipes from amazon, and she was also a good cook.

Ihre Eltern hatten für moderne Küchen nicht viel übrig. Wozu auch? Zum Essen gab es immer Deutsche **Hausmannskost,** die wie üblich bestehend aus Kartoffeln, Bohnen, Wurst und groben Zutaten bestand.
Da Lena schon Anfang dreißig war, **erwartete ihre Familie**, dass sie endlich einen festen deutschen Partner findet, heiratet und eine Familie gründet. Es gab nur ein Problem für Lena.
Sie hatte keine Arbeit, und wie überall, Arbeitslosigkeit macht das Leben kompliziert.

Her parents weren't interested in modern kitchens. However, why? They always ate American plain meals that usually consisted of fries, beans, sausages and coarse ingredients. Because Lena was already thirty years old, her family did expect that she finally found a partner, married and founded a family. But there was a problem for Lena. She didn't have work and unemployment makes life difficult, as everywhere.

Arbeit oder nicht, eine Küche musste her! Sechshundert Euro hatte sie gespart. Um die Ecke gab es einen großen **Baumarkt** der montags immer **Angebote** für Küchen hatte. Aber das war nicht alles. Baumärkte sind in Deutschland Plätze, wo man häufig Nachbarn und Freunde traf.
Am Montagmorgen stand Lena vor dem **Haupteingang** und wartete.

With or without work, she needed that kitchen! She had saved six hundred dollars. Around the corner was a huge home center which always had discounts for kitchens on Mondays. But that wasn't all. Hardware stores, just like supermarkets, can be places where you can often meet neighbors and friends. On Monday morning Lena stood in front of the main entrance and waited.

Und tatsächlich, nach schon zwanzig Minuten kam die erste Nachbarin. Lena zögerte nicht. Sie sagte der älteren Dame, sie müsse unbedingt einen **Schnellkochtopf** kaufen, der alte sei gerade **kaputtgegangen**, und jetzt fehlen ihr noch dreißig Euro für einen neuen Topf. Nach einer weiteren Minute Unterhaltung gab die Dame ihr das Geld.

Es klappte wunderbar, Lena traf noch ein halbes Dutzend **Nachbarn und Bekannte**, gegen Mittag hatte sie das Geld für die neue Küche zusammen.

Indeed, after twenty minutes the first neighbor came. Lena didn't hesitate. She told the old woman that she urgently needed to buy a pressure cooker because the old one was broken, and she needed thirty dollars for a new pot. After a while the woman gave her the money. It perfectly worked; Lena met half a dozen neighbours and acquaintances, and on midday she had enough money for the new kitchen.

Zusammenfassung

Lena wohnt noch bei ihren Eltern im Dachgeschoss und braucht eine neue Küche. Da sie arbeitslos ist, hat sie kein Geld sich eine zu kaufen. Lena braucht Hilfe. Sie geht zum Baumarkt und sagt fremden Leuten, sie brauche heute noch einen neuen Schnellkochtopf, und es fehlt nur noch ein bisschen Geld. Viele Leute schenken ihr Geld.

Vokabeln

anzuschaffen / anschaffen I to acquire something

Dachgeschoss attic

Kochnische I kitchenette

gestöbert / stöbern to rummage

Angebote specials/discounts

Hausmannskost plain meals

..erwartete ihre Familie ..did her family expect

Arbeitslosigkeit unemployment

Baumarkt I home center

Haupteingang I main entrance

Schnellkochtopf pressure cooker

kaputtgegangen / kaputtgehen to get broken / got broken

Nachbarn und Bekannte I neighbors and acquaintances

Beantworte die folgenden Fragen im Auswahlverfahren. Nur eine Antwort je Frage ist richtig

1. Was gab es im Dachgeschoss?
a) Eine Toilette
b) Eine Kochnische
c) Eine neue Küche
d) Alte Kochbücher

2. Was konnte man montags immer im Baumarkt finden?
a) Neue Küchen b) Nachbarn und Freunde
c) Angebote für Küchen
d) Musik

3. Was sagte Lena, als sie vor dem Baumarkt stand?
a) Sie braucht eine neue Küche
b) Sie will heiraten
c) Sie ist arbeitslos
d) Sie braucht einen neuen Schnellkochtopf

4. Wann hatte Lena das Geld für eine neue Küche zusammen?
a) Gegen Mittag
b) Gegen Abend
c) Am nächsten Tag
d) Nach einer Stunde

Lösungen
1b 2c 3d 4a

AUDIO (copy and paste into your browser)

http://bit.ly/2IdmT1k

Die Frau die eine Spionin war

The woman who was a spy

Viele Leute im Dorf glaubten, Karin kommt aus Berlin, Deutschlands **Hauptstadt.** Die Leute sagten auch, sie spreche mit Akzent, und viele ältere Leute sagten sogar, sie komme wohl aus Rumänien.

The people in the village thought that Karin comes from Berlin, Germany's capital. The people also said that she was speaking with an accent, and many elderly people even said, that she probably came from Romania.

Karin ging **regelmäßig** in ein China Restaurant zum Essen, dort erfuhr man, wer sich für sie interessierte, sie lebe mit ihrer **erwachsenen Tochter**, eine junge Frau die angeblich ab nächsten Sommer nach Berlin geht, um dort zu studieren. Man weiß, Karin hatte auch einen Dachshund namens Max, mit den sie wohl mindestens einmal pro Tag **spazieren ging**. Sie hatte auch Geld, glaubten die meisten, aber arbeiten ging sie nicht. Karin hatte ein **offenes Geheimnis**, sie trank gerne Wein. Ein bis zwei Flaschen Rotwein am Tag, sie bevorzugte den Wein allein zu trinken.

Karin went regularly to a Chinese restaurant and there everyone, who was interested in her, could hear that she lives with her grown up daughter, a young woman who allegedly goes to Berlin next summer to study. It's also known that Karin owns a dachshund named Max, with whom she takes a walk at least once a day. She also had money, most of the people thought but she didn't work. Karin had an open secret, she loved drinking wine. One to two bottles of red wine per day and she preferred to drink the wine alone.

Am frühen Nachmittag fing sie an zu trinken und bis abends trank sie weiter.
Besser als in Kneipen gehen und dort **den Ruf** zu verlieren, dachte sie. Teilweise hatte sie ihren Ruf schon verloren, denn im lokalen Aldi Supermarkt sah man sie regelmäßig **den Einkaufswagen** voll mit Weinflaschen.
Was den ganzen Ort interessierte, war, was machte sie wirklich, warum wollte sie alleine leben? Sie schien auch häufig länger verreist zu sein.

In the early afternoon, she began to drink and continued drinking until evening started.
Better than going in the pub and losing her reputation there, she thought. She partly had lost her reputation because in the local supermarket Aldi she could regularly be seen with a shopping cart full of wine bottles.
What the people were interested in, was what kind of work she had, and why she lives alone. She also seemed to travel alot.

Ein Tag vor Weihnachten hielt ein dunkler Wagen vor ihrem Wohnhaus. Männer und Frauen in Uniform. War es die Polizei? Wir wussten es nicht.
Interessanterweise, hielt ein paar Tage später wieder **ein Fahrzeug** vor der Tür. Diesmal ein weißer Van. Karin hatte an diesen dunklen Wintertag eine Sonnenbrille auf, und stieg **hastig** in das Fahrzeug, und der Wagen entschwand.

Ein Nachbar behauptete das Fahrzeug hatte **ausländische Kennzeichen** mit einer kleinen blau-weißer Fahne darauf.

One day before Christmas a dark vehicle parked in front of her house. Men and women in uniforms; was it the police? We didn't know.
Interestingly a few days later another vehicle parked in front of the door. This time it was a white Van. Karin wore on this dark winter's day her sunglasses and got hastily inside the vehicle and the car disappeared. A neighbor claimed that the car had has had foreign plates with a tiny blue-white flag on it.

Zusammenfassung

Karin lebt in einer Kleinstadt. Die Leute sagen, sie sei eine Trinkerin, denn sie kauft oft Alkohol. Eines Tages kommen Uniformierte, und kurze Zeit später wird sie von unbekannten Fremden abgeholt. Die Fremden scheinen einer ausländischen Organisation anzugehören.

Vokabeln

die alte TrinkerinI old drunkard / old lush

unbedeutende Stadt *insignificant town*

regelmäßig I *regularly*

erwachsene Tochter I *grown up daughter*

spazieren gehen *taking a walk*

offenes Geheimnis *open secret*

der Ruf I *reputation*

ein Fahrzeug *vehicle*

der Einkaufswagen I *shopping cart*

hastig I *hurried*

ausländische Kennzeichen I *foreign plates*

Beantworte die folgenden Fragen im Auswahlverfahren. Nur eine Antwort je Frage ist richtig

1. Was sagten die alten Leute über Karin?

a) Sie kommt aus Rumänien

b) Sie sucht einen Mann

c) Sie sucht eine neue Arbeit

d) Sie kommt aus Pinneberg

2. Was war Karins offene Geheimnis?
a) Sie reiste viel
b) Sie trank gerne Rotwein
c) Sie hatte eine Tochter
d) Sie war schwanger

3. Was passierte ein Tag vor Weihnachten?
a) Ein dunkler Wagen hielt vor dem Wohnhaus
b) Ihr Sohn kam zu Besuch
c) Karin trank Rotwein
d) Ein Nachbar rief die Polizei

4. Was behauptete ein Nachbar?
a) Karin ist eine Alkoholikerin
b) Karin ist eine Spionin
c) Ihr Sohn kam und holte sie ab

Lösungen
1a 2b 3a 4b

AUDIO (copy and paste into your browser)

http://bit.ly/2UbFmNv

Schifffahrt Romantik

Ship Romance

Mein Name ist Anna und morgen geht es los. Koffer packen sind kein Kinderspiel, und obwohl ich mich seit Wochen darauf **vorbereitet** habe, habe ich im Moment Probleme einen klaren Kopf zu behalten. Ich muss genau wissen, was ich **mitnehmen** muss und was zu Hause bleibt. Ich habe gerade gelesen, dass ich keine Flaschen und **Lebensmittel** mitnehmen darf.

My name is Anna and it all begins tomorrow. Packing the luggage is no cakewalk and although I've been preparing for weeks I currently have problems to keep a clear head. I need to know exactly what I have to prepare and what I have to leave at home. I have just read that I mustn't take any bottles or groceries with me. The cruise starts in Italy. There are no real cruises starting in Germany except on rivers such as the Danube or the Rhein, but they are exclusively for retirees.

Die Kreuzfahrt startet von Italien aus. Von Deutschland aus, gibt es keine richtigen Kreuzfahrten, außer auf Flüssen wie auf der Donau oder dem Rhein, die aber **ausschließlich** für Rentner sind. Meine Kreuzfahrt geht morgen Abend los.
Es ist ein riesiges Schiff, mit mehreren Schwimmbädern und vielen Restaurants. **Der Gedanke**, eine Schiffsreise als Urlaub zu buchen, kam mir, als ich neulich eine alte Freundin wieder traf. Sie hatte es schon über Facebook verbreitet, sie hatte endlich ihren **Traummann** gefunden.

The cruise starts in Italy. There are no real cruises starting in Germany except river cruises like they have on the Danube or Rhine, but they are exclusively for retirees. My vacation on a cruise ship begins tomorrow in the evening.
It's an enormous vessel with several swimming pools and lots of restaurants. The thought to book a cruise for vacation came to my mind when I lately met an old friend. She had already spread the news on Facebook that she has finally found her dream man.

So schön kann das Leben sein. Zehn Jahre Online Dating und dann hat meine kleine **übergewichtige Freundin** tatsächlich einen Freund gefunden. Muss ein **reicher Kerl** sein, jetzt weiß ich, was so eine Kreuzfahrt kostet.
Über fünftausend Euro hat meine Reise gekostet, aber die Reise meiner Freundin muss noch teurer gewesen sein. Meine Gedanken wandern zwischen packen und schicken Männern, Cocktails und Hygiene-Artikel. Diese sollte man lieber **reichlich dabeihaben.**
Tampons und Shampoos wiegen zum Glück nicht viel.

Ich höre die Tür klingeln. Wer kann das jetzt sein, ich habe keine Zeit!
Life can be that beautiful. After ten years of online dating my overweight female friend has finally found a boyfriend. He must be a rich guy; now I know how much such a cruise trips costs. My trip had cost over five thousand Euros, but my friends voyage must have been even more expensive. My thoughts are wandering between packing and posh guys, cocktails and toiletries. It's better to have plenty of them.

Tampons and shampoos fortunately don't weigh a lot. I hear the doorbell ringing. Who might that be, I have no time!

"Hallo Andrea! Welch **eine Überraschung**!"
"Hallo Anna, ich wollte dich nur mal kurz grüßen bevor morgen du morgen deine Kreuzfahrt antrittst. Darf ich dir meinen **Verlobten** vorstellen. Hier, das ist Bobi aus Manila"
"Angenehm"
"Hi!"
"Spricht er auch Deutsch?"
"Nein, aber sehr gut Englisch. Er hat schließlich auf der Kreuzfahrt, wo ich ihn kennengelernt habe, gearbeitet. **Er war dort Kellner**. Er ist ein ganz fähiger Mann!"
Hello, Andrea! What a surprise!"
"Hello Anna, I just wanted to say a last time hello before you'll start your cruise trip tomorrow. May I introduce you to my fiancé. This is Bobo from Manila."
"I'm pleased to meet you"
"Hi!"
"Does he speak English as well?"
"He speaks English very well. After all he had worked on the cruise ship, where I met him. He was a waiter there. He is a quite capable man!"

Zusammenfassung

Anna plant eine Kreuzfahrt. Sie hofft dort einen Mann kennenzulernen. Ihre Freundin war auch auf einer Kreuzfahrt und hat dort ihren Verlobten, einen Kellner kennengelernt.

Vokabeln

vorbereiten I *to prepare*

mitnehmen I *take / to take so/s.th.*

Lebensmittel *groceries*

ausschließlich *exclusively*

der Gedanke *the thought*

der Traummann *dream man*

übergewichtige Freundin

overweight female friend

reicher Kerl I *rich guy*

eine Uberraschung *a surprise*

Verlobter I *fiance*

er war dort Kellner I *he was a waiter there*

Beantworte die folgenden Fragen im Auswahlverfahren. Nur eine Antwort je Frage ist richtig

1. Von wo aus startet die geplante Kreuzfahrt?

a) von Italien
b) von Deutschland
c) von England
d) von Amerika

2. Was hat die übergewichtige Freundin gemacht ,um einen Freund zu finden?

a) Sie hat Diat gemacht
b) Sie ist gereist
c) Sie hat es zehn Jahre online versucht.
d) Sie hat gar nichts gemacht.

3. Wie viel Euro hat die Reise gekostet?

a) Die Reise war umsonst
b) Uber fünftausend Euro
c) Die Reise war ein Geschenk der Freundin
d) Uber tausend Euro

4. Welchen Beruf hat der Verlobte von Annas Freundin?

a) Busfahrer
b) Kellner
c) arbeitslos
d) Lehrer

Lösungen

1 a 2 c 3 b 4 b

AUDIO (copy and paste into your browser)

http://bit.ly/2KuvBdH

Das Jagdmesser

The hunting knife

Mark und Emma haben Kinder die noch im Haus leben, **das Ehepaar** lebt aber seit kurzem **getrennt**. Mark hat zum Glück noch eine kleine Wohnung in der Stadt und hat das Familienhaus Emma und den Kindern **überlassen**. Die Eltern von Emma sind beide schon Ende siebzig und haben am Wochenende **Silberhochzeit**.

Mark and Emma have children who still live in their house, but the couple has been separated for a short time. Fortunately, Mark still has a little flat in the city and has left the house to Emma and the children. Emma's' parents are both already close to eighty years and are feasting their silver wedding anniversary at the weekend.

Es ist soweit ein herrlicher, warmer Sommer, und der Vater von Emma, Heinz hat eine Idee. Warum nicht einen schönen **Grillabend** im Garten von Mark veranstalten. Freunde, die Kinder und **Verwandte**, alle würden sie kommen. Außerdem hat sich Heinz schon immer mit Mark gut verstanden. Beide sind schließlich **Jäger** im Jagdclub. Trennung oder nicht, es würde ein guter Grill-Abend werden. Heinz ruft seine Tochter an, und erwartet eine **Zusage** für das Wochenende. Es kostet Emma viel **Überzeugung**, dass ausgerechnet Mark auf seinen eigenen Grundstück den Grill-Meister spielen soll.
Mark sagt zu.

A beautiful, warm summer and Emma's father Heinz has an idea. Why shouldn't they arrange a barbecue evening in the garden of *Mark. Friends, the kids and relatives – all of them would come. Furthermore, Heinz has always liked Mark. After all they are both hunters in a hunting club. Break-up or not, it would be a great barbecue evening. Heinz calls his daughter and expects a promise for the weekend. It costs Emma a lot of conviction that Mark, of all people, should play the barbecue master in his own garden. Mark agrees.*

Samstagnachmittag ist es soweit. Der Grill wird zum Glühen gebracht, Würste und Schweinefleisch werden auf dem Grill gelegt, die Kinder spielen, die Erwachsenen trinken Bier und Musik dröhnt aus einer alten Stereoanlage. Heinz hilft Mark am Grill, obwohl es ihm körperlich **schwer fällt.** Heute hat seine Brille vergessen. Plötzlich fällt Mark ein, er hat noch ein **Geschenk** für Heinz.
Schnell läuft er zum Wagen und holt eine Schatulle, die er Heinz überreicht. Heinz staunt nicht schlecht, als er sein Geschenk aufmacht. Ein großes **Jagdmesser** mit Horngriff!
Mark erklärt, dies sei ein ganz **besonderes** Messer der **Traditionsmarke** Puma aus Solingen. Ein Messer für **Sammler!**

Saturday in the afternoon it's time to start. The grill is heated, sausages and pork are placed on the grill, the children are playing and the adults are drinking beer and music is blasting out an old stereo. Heinz helps Mark at the grill although it is physically difficult for him. He had forgotten his glasses. Suddenly it comes into Mark' mind that he has a present for Heinz.

He quickly runs to the car and gets a casket which he hands over to Heinz.
Heinz is quite surprised when he opens his present. It's a big hunting knife with a horn handle!
Mark explains that this was a very special knife by a traditional knifemaker of the brand Puma from Solingen. A knife for collectors!

Der schöne Abend geht zu Ende. Als Mark gehen will, gibt Emma ihm noch einen Kuss, und sagt ihm, sie möchte ihn morgen sprechen. Am Sonntag treffen sich Mark und Emma. Sie ist ihm immer noch sehr **dankbar** für den tollen Grillabend. Beide haben eine Unterhaltung, Mark sagt ihr, in der alten Beziehung war nicht alles schlecht. Emma macht Mark den **Vorschlag**, sie könnten wegen der Kinder wieder **zusammenleben**.
Tatsächlich zieht die Familie schon eine Woche später wieder zusammen. Mark ist besonders glücklich, zumal das billige, gefälschte Messer vom **Markt** in Thailand wohl seine Wirkung nicht verfehlte.

The beautiful evening has come to an end. When Mark is about to leave, Emma gives him a kiss and says that she wants to talk to him the next day.
On Sunday Mark and Emma meet again. She feels still very thankful for the splendid barbecue evening.
They have a conversation and Mark tells her, that during their relationship not everything has been bad. Emma makes a proposal to Mark; for the children they could live together again.

Indeed, after one week the family moves again together. Mark is very happy, especially because the cheap fake knife from a market in Thailand didn't fail to make an impression.

Zusammenfassung

Mark und Emma haben sich getrennt. Wegen der Silberhochzeit ihrer Eltern veranstaltet sie einen Grillabend der ganzen Familie. Mark schenkt Emmas Vater ein besonderes Jagdmesser. Emma freut sich sehr, und zieht wieder mit Mark zusammen. Das Jagdmesser hat Mark im Urlaub in Thailand gekauft.

Vokabeln

das Ehepaar *the couple*
getrennt *separated*
überlassen *to leave / surrender*
die Verwandte *relatives*
Der Grillabend *barbeque evening*
Der Jäger *hunter*
die Zusage *promise*
die Überzeugung *conviction*
schwerfallen s.th. is difficult to do
Geschenk *gift / present*
das Jagdmesser *hunting knife*
besonders *special*
die Traditionsmarke *traditional brand*
der Sammler *collector*
dankbar *thankful*
der Vorschlag *proposal*
der Markt *market*

Beantworte die folgenden Fragen im Auswahlverfahren.
Nur eine Antwort je Frage ist richtig

1. Was planen die Eltern von Emma am Wochenende?
a) die Silberhochzeit
b) eine Reise
c) eine Hochzeit
d) den Besuch ihrer Tochter

2. Warum sagt Mark, dass Jagdmesser ist ein besonderes Messer?
a) Weil es ein Jagdmesser ist
b) Weil es ein Tradionsmesser aus Solingen ist
c) Weil es ein Geschenk ist
d) Weil es billig war

3. Wie ist die Reaktion Emmas auf den Grillabend?
a) Sie ist Mark dankbar.
b) Sie ist krank geworden
c) Sie plant einen weiteren Grillabend
d) Sie zieht zu ihren Eltern

4. Warum ist Mark nach dem Grillabend besonders glücklich?
a) Weil er Emma heiratet wird
b) Weil er das Messer billig gekauft hat.
c) Weil er nach Thailand reist
d) Weil er der Grillmeister war.

Lösungen
1a 2b 3a 4b

AUDIO (copy and paste into your browser)

http://bit.ly/2VztrKS

Besuch aus Amerika

A Visit from America

Irma und Paul sind **Rentner**, sie kommen **ursprünglich** aus Hamburg, verbringen aber die meiste Zeit in Bayern, ein Bundesland in Süddeutschland. Schon vor vielen Jahren hatten sie sich in einem Dorf ein **Landhaus** gekauft.
Das Ehepaar kommt aus **einfachen Verhältnissen**. Paul war früher **Busfahrer**, seine Frau Irma hat früher in Supermärkten gearbeitet. Beide sind nicht gebildet, wollen es auch nicht sein, aber sie sind **glücklich**, denn beide sind gesund, und sie können sich ein schönes Haus in Bayern leisten.
Eines Nachmittags klingelt die Tür.

Irma and Paul are pensioners, they are originally from Hamburg but they are spending most of their time in Bavaria, a state in South Germany. For many years, they had bought a country house in a village.
The couple comes from humble homes. Paul worked as a bus driver and his wife Irma worked in a supermarket. Both of them are not intellectual, but they also don't want to and are happy, because both of them are healthy and they can afford a nice house in Bavaria. One afternoon the doorbell rings.

Paul öffnet die Tür und vor ihnen steht ein Mann mit zwei Kindern. **Unbekannte** Menschen.
"Guten Tag, was kann ich für sie tun?"
Der Mann antwortet in einer **Sprache**, die er nicht versteht. Paul ruft seine Frau. Irma begrüßt die Leute, die alle enthusiastisch

und erfreut durcheinander reden, ohne das Irma und Paul ein davon Wort verstehen.

"Ich glaube die sprechen Englisch", sagt Irma zu Willi.
Paul opens the door and in front of him stands a man with two children. Strangers.
"Good day, how can I help you?" Paul asks.
The man answers in a language that he doesn't understand. Pau calls his wife. Irma greets the people who are talking enthusiastically but Irma and Paul don't understand a word.
"I think they are speaking English", Irma says.

Die fremden Kinder nicken, fast scheinen sie zu **jubeln**.
Plötzlich greift der fremde Mann in seiner Tasche und holt ein altes schwarz-weißes Foto raus. Er zeigt es Paul und Irma. Pau setzt sich eine Brille auf und **nickt freundlich**.
Die fremde Familie jubelt, die Kinder umarmen Willi.
Ohne zu **zögern**, stürmt die fremde Familie ins Haus. Sie reden laut in ihrer Sprache und scheinen sich sehr zu freuen. Der Mann zeigt auf eine Kuckucksuhr, und dann mit einem Finger auf seine Brust.
Irma lächelt. "So was hat er wohl auch."

The strange children nod and seem almost to cheer.
Suddenly the strange man grabs his bag and takes out a black and white photograph. He reveals it to Irma and Willi. Paul puts on his glasses and nods friendly.
The strange family cheers and the children are hugging Willi.
Without hesitation the strange family storms into the house. They are talking in their own language and seem to be more

than happy. The man points at the cuckoo clock and then he points with his finger at his chest.
Irma smiles. "He seems to own the same."

Die Kinder gehen in die Küche und öffnen den Kühlschrank.
Irma und Paul folgen ihnen.
"**Seid ihr hungrig**", fragt Irma. "Wir haben heute Sauerkraut mit Wurst, ich mache euch das Essen warm"
Die Kinder **umarmen** Irma, der Fremde Mann schüttelt Paul die Hand. Am Tisch wird gegessen, gelacht, und plötzlich versteht Paul einige Wörter der Fremden.
Amerika, Großvater! Paul und Irma nicken freundlich, die fremde Leute sprechen alle durcheinander.

The children go in the kitchen and open the fridge.
Irma and Paul follow them.
"Are you hungry" asks Irma. "Today we have sauerkraut with sausage. I'll warm it up for you."
The children hug Irma and the strange man shakes Willis' hand. At the table they eat and laugh and suddenly Paul understands a few words of the strangers.
"America, grandfather!" Paul and Irma are nodding friendly, the strangers speak all at once.

Plötzlich steht die fremde Familie auf, sie umarmen Irma und Willi. Zum Abschied überreicht der fremde Mann Paul das alte Foto. Wille nickt freundlich. Dann ist die Familie fort. Paul schaut nochmals auf das alte Foto, schüttelt den Kopf und sagt zu Irma: "Das muss der alte **Eigentümer** sein, als er noch jung war."
"Ja, aber **wer waren diese Leute** denn", fragt Irma.

All of a sudden the strange family stands up and hug Irma and Willi. On parting the strange man hands the photograph to Willi. Paul nods friendly. Then the family is gone. Paullooks again at the picture and says to Irma: "That might be the old proprietary when he was young."
"Yes, but who were these people?"

Zusammenfassung

Paul und seine Frau Irma sind Rentner und leben in einem Landhaus. Sie bekommen Besuch einer fremden Familie, die kein Deutsch spricht. Die Familie geht ins Haus und versuchen sich mit den Rentnern zu unterhalten. Die Fremden sind erfreut und aufgeregt. Nach dem Essen gehen sie wieder, Paul und Irma wissen nicht, wer sie waren.'

Vokabeln

der Rentner *pensioners / retirees*

ursprünglich *originally*

das Landhaus *country house*

einfache Verhältnisse f
rom humble homes

der Busfahrer *bus driver*

glücklich *happy*

unbekannte *unknown*

Sprache *language*

jubeln *cheer*

plötzlich *suddenly*

zögern *hesitate*

seid ihr hungrig *are you hungry?*

umarmen *to embrace / hug*

Eigentümer *proprietary / owner*

wer waren diese Leute? who were these people?

Beantworte die folgenden Fragen im Auswahlverfahren. Nur eine Antwort je Frage ist richtig

1. Was hat Irma gemacht, bevor sie in Rente ging?

a) Sie hat in Supermärkten gearbeitet
b) Sie hat auf einem Bauernhof gearbeitet
c) Sie war Hausfrau
d) Sie hat im Ausland gelebt

2. Was holt der fremde Mann aus seiner Tasche?

a) Eine Pistole
b) Einen Umschlag mit Geld drin, denn er wollte das Haus kaufen
c) Ein Foto
d) Ein Geschenk

3. Was bietet Irma den Kindern im Haus an?

a) Eine Kuckucksuhr
b) Warmes Essen

c) Ein Foto des Hauses
d) Einen Umschlag mit Geld drin

4. Als die fremde Familie wieder geht, was machen sie zum Schluss?
a) Sie umarmen Paul und Irma
b) Sie schenken Paul und Irma Geld
c) Sie geben Paul und Irma einen Umschlag
d) Sie gehen ohne etwas zu tun oder zu sagen.

Lösungen
1 a
2 c
3 b
4 d

AUDIO (copy and paste into your browser)

http://bit.ly/2GiJgk8

Der Schatz im Wald

The treasure in the woods

Jan Meyer war ein romantischer Mensch. Obwohl er **damals** schon 18 Jahre alt war, interessierte er sich mehr an Fantasien aus **Geschichtsbüchern**, als an junge Mädchen, anders als seine Freunde oder **Klassenkamerade**n.
Wenn er nicht schlief oder mit Hausaufgaben **beschäftig**t war, **döste** auf dem Sofa, und träumte davon eines Tages reich zu sein. Einen nachmittags schlief er auf dem Sofa komplett ein. Er hatte **einen lebhaften Traum**.

Jan Meyer is a romantic person. Although he has been already 18 years old at that time, he was more interested in history books than in young ladies, other than his friends and classmates.
When he didn't sleep or wasn't busy with his homework he used to doze on the sofa and was dreaming of having lots of money one day. One afternoon he fell asleep on the couch. He had a lively dream.

Er träumte einen Schatz auf einer Insel gefunden zu haben. Als er eine alte **Truhe** fand, öffnete er sie, und eine Wolke aus **Rauch** stieg daraus hervor. Der Rauch formte sich zum Gesicht, und eine alte **Stimme** sagte: "Steh auf, geh in den Wald, dort findest du eine Karte. Die Karte wird neben einer alten Pinien-Tanne begraben sein. Grabe ein Loch wo du Rauch aufsteigen siehst. Es ist Eine **Schatzkarte.** Eine Stimme sagte: Du kannst reich werden, wenn du die Karte findest.

He dreamed to have found a treasure on an island. As he found the chest, he opened it and a little cloud of smoke came out. The smoke formed itself to a mouth and an old voice said: Get up, go to the forest, you'll find a map there. The map will be buried beneath an old pine tree. Dig a hole where you'll see some smoke fuming. It's a treasure map. A voice said: You can become rich if you find the map.

Der Rauch näherte sich seinem **Gesicht**, Jan konnte plötzlich nicht mehr **atmen**, er glaubte zu ersticken.
Jan, erinnerte sich, heute ist Sonntag, es musste schon **nachmittags** sein.
Draußen war es schon Herbst, Nebel lag über dem Land. Gleich hinter dem Haus war ein Pfad, der direkt in den Wald führte. Er folgte den Pfand und keine hundert Meter gegangen, sah er die Pinien Tanne, und daneben stieg ein feiner, weißer Rauch gerade in den Himmel.

The smoke came closer to his face, all of a sudden Jan couldn't breathe anymore, and he thought to be choking.
Jan remembered that this day was Sunday and it must already have been afternoon.
It was already autumn, fog laid over the landscape. Behind the house a path began, which lead directly to the forest. He followed the track and he didn't even go one hundred meters, as he already saw the pine tree and beside he could see fine, white smoke rising to the sky.

Jan **buddelte im Boden**, und fand ein kleines Rohr, **im Inneren** fand er eine zusammengerollte **Schriftrolle**.

Es sah aus wie eine Buddhistische Karte oder Schriftrolle. Er rollte sie zusammen und ging nach Hause.

Jan dug into the soil and found a little tube and inside he found a rolled-up scroll.
It looked like a Buddhist map or a scroll. He rolled it up and went home.

Am folgenden Tag ging er gleich nach der Schule in ein Geschäft, das Gold und Wertgegenstände kauft. Für die Karte gab es kein Geld. Jan ging nach Hause, legte sich auf das Sofa und schlief ein. Er träumte, dass er nie wieder Geld brauchte. Als er aufwachte, blickte er lächelnd auf die Schatzkarte. Das Geld und der Schatz waren nicht mehr wichtig.

The next day he went directly after school to a shop, where gold and other objects of value could be sold. He didn't get any money for the map. John went home, lied on the couch and fell asleep. He dreamed that he would never need any money. As he woke up he glanced smiling at the treasure map. The money and the treasure weren't important to him anymore.

Zusammenfassung

Jan ist ein verträumter junger Mann. Eines Tages träumt er davon, dass er einen Schatz im Wald finden wird. Als wer aufwacht, versucht er den Schatz zu finden. Er findet im Wald eine Schriftrolle. Danach möchte er keinen Schatz mehr finden und auch nicht mehr reich sein.

Vokabeln

damals *at that time*

Geschichtsbücher *history books*

Klassenkameraden *classmates*

beschäftigen / beschäftigt *to occupy so.*

dösen / döste *to doze / dozed*

die Truhe *chest / coffer*

einen lebhaften Traum *a lively dream*

der Rauch *to smoke*

die Stimme *voice*

eine Schatzkarte *a treasure map*

das Gesicht *face*

atmen *to breathe*

nachmittags *afternoon*

buddelte im Boden *digged into the soil*

Beantworte die folgenden Fragen im Auswahlverfahren. Nur eine Antwort je Frage ist richtig

1. Wofür interessierte sich Jan?
a) Für Kochbücher
b) Für Geschichtsbücher
c) Für seine Klassenkameraden
d) Für Reisen

2. Wo lag die Karte begraben?
a) Neben einer Pinien-Tanne
b) Unter dem Haus
c) Auf dem Friedhof
d) Nirgendwo

3. Was fand Jan Mueller im Boden?
a) Eine Schatztruhe
b) Ein Rohr mit einer Schriftrolle
c) Geld
d) Eine Buddha Statue

Lösungen
1 b 2 a 3 b

AUDIO (copy and paste into your browser)

http://bit.ly/2VEa971

Die Putzfrau

The maid

Marta kommt aus Polen und **arbeite**t zweimal die Woche **als Putzfrau** in einem großen Haus. Das Haus gehört Frau Schuh, die allein lebt. Ab und zu kommt ihr Sohn **zu Besuch.** Ihr Sohn ist arbeitslos und bekommt Geld von der Mutter.

Marta comes from Poland and works twice a week as charlady in a big house. The house belongs to Frau Schuh, who is living alone. Once in a while her son comes for a visit. Her son is unemployed and receives some money from his mother.

Der Sohn lebt bei einem Freund. Er kommt oft **in den Morgenstunden** zum Haus seiner Mutter und **schaut Fernsehen**. Wenn das Wetter gut ist, sitzt er auf Terrasse und trinkt Bier. Marta muss die leeren Bierflaschen in den Keller bringen. Im Keller liegen noch **riesige Mengen** an Kisten mit vollen Bierflaschen. Der Sohn kauft das Bier im **Großhandel**.

The son lives at a friends' place. He often comes in the morning hours to his mother house and is watching TV. If the weather is fine, he sits on the terrace and drinks beer. Marta has to carry the empty beer bottles in the basement. In the basement are still huge numbers of cases with full beer bottles storing. The son orders the beer at a wholesaler

Frau Schuh arbeitet sehr hart. Sie arbeitet in einer Fabrik und **kommt spät nach Hause**. Aber sie ruft oft ihren Sohn an und manchmal auch Marta.

Eines Tages bittet der Sohn Marta um **einen Gefallen**. Er sagt. " Ich reise für einige Wochen nach Spanien. Sagen Sie es nicht meiner Mutter. Lassen Sie alles normal erscheinen.
"Kein Problem", sagt Marta.

Frau Schuh works very hard. She works in a factory and comes home very late. But she often calls her son and also sometimes Marta.
One day the son ask Marta for a favor. He says: "I'll make a trip to Spain for a few weeks. Don't tell it my mother. Make it appear as everything would be normal.
"No problem", says Marta.

Die folgenden Tage scheint alles normal zu sein. Frau Schuh ruft Marta an und fragt, ob ihr Sohn zu Hause ist, und ob sonst alles normal ist.
"Ja Frau Schuh, alles ist in Ordnung." Marta sitzt auf der Terrasse und trinkt Bier. Sie wird die leeren Flaschen **in den Keller bringen.**

The next days everything seems to be normal. Frau Schuh calls Marta and asks her whether her son was at home and whether everything was in order.
"Yes, Frau Schuh, everything is alright." Marta is sitting on the terrace and drinking beer. She'll carry the empty bottles into the basement.

Zusammenfassung

Eine polnische Putzfrau arbeitet im Haus von Frau Schuh. Wenn Frau Schuh nicht zu Hause ist, Ihr Sohn kommt sie manchmal besuchen um auf der Terrasse Bier zu trinken. Er hat viel Bier im Keller gelagert. Der Sohn sagt der Putzfrau, sie solle ein Geheimnis bewahren , das er nach Spanien fliegt, Alles soll normal erscheinen. Deshalb sagt die Putzfrau nichts und trinkt sein Bier.

Vokabeln

Fernsehen schauen watching TV

riesige Mengen huge amounts

der Grosshandel wholesale

spät nach Hause kommen coming home late

einen Gefallen a favour

in den Keller brigen to bring (s.th.) into the basement

Beantworte die folgenden Fragen im Auswahlverfahren. Nur eine Antwort je Frage ist richtig

1. Was macht der Sohn wenn er ins Haus kommt?
a) Er kocht Mittagessen
b) Er trinkt Bier
c) Er guckt Fernsehen
d) Er surft im Internet

2. Was lagert im Keller?
a) Kisten mit Lebensmittel
b) Ein Fernseher
c) Leere Bierflaschen
d) Kisten mit vollen Bierflaschen

3. Was macht Marta beruflich?
a) Sie ist Hausfrau
b) Marta ist arbeitslos
c) Marta arbeitet in einer Fabrik
d) Marta arbeitet in einem Restaurant

4. Welchen Plan hat Martas Sohn?
a) Er will nach Spanien verreisen
b) Er will das Bier aus dem Keller holen
c) Er versucht Arbeit zu finden.
d) Er mochte Marta helfen

Lösungen
1b 2c 3c 4a

AUDIO (copy and paste into your browser)

http://bit.ly/2VDK48j

Der Schrebergarten

Deutschland ist bekannt für seine Schrebergärten**. Außerhalb der großen Städte** findet man Gebiete mit vielen kleine Gärten. In jedem Garten steht **eine kleine Hütte.** Viele dieser Gärten bilden eine kleine Kolonie.

Diese Gärten und Hütten nennt man Schrebergärten. Die meisten kann man kaufen. **Die Eigentümer sind meistens Rentner**. **Die Rentner freuen sich im Garten zu arbeiten**. Einer dieser Schrebergärten gehört Rainer Voigt, einen Rentner aus Hamburg. Außerhalb Hamburgs hat er sich einen Schrebergarten gekauft. In seinem Garten befindet sich **ein kleiner Teich**. Im Teich schwimmen kleine Goldfische.

Herr Voigt ist auch Angler. **Er kennt sich mit Fischen aus**. Herr Meier hat keine Familie und liebt seine Fische. **Jeden Fisch hat er einen Namen gegeben**.

Eines Tages besucht Herr Voigt seinen Schrebergarten. Zwei Fische liegen an der Oberfläche. Die Fische sind tot. Später findet Herr Voigt noch mehr tote Fische. Dafür gibt es keine **Erklärung**. Herr Voigt ist sehr traurig. **Er entscheidet** sich den

Schrebergarten zu verkaufen. Obwohl er eine Anzeige aufgibt, kauft keiner seinen Schrebergarten. Aber Herr Voigt ist mit vielen **Nachbarn** befreundet. **Nach kurzer Zeit** verschenkt Herr Voigt seinen Schrebergarten an einem Nachbarn.

Die Nachbarn **übernehmen** den Schrebergarten, und sind glücklich mit ihrem **Geschenk**. Schon nach kurzer Zeit befindet sich alles **im hervorragendem Zustand**. Der Garten **blüht,** und im Teich schwimmen viele Fische.

Ab und zu, kommt Herr Voigt zu Besuch. Er möchte sehen, was sich in seinem alten Schrebergarten verändert hat. Der Schrebergarten sieht **sehr gepflegt** aus, und Herr Voigt ist neidisch. Eines Tages liegen wieder tote Fische im Teich. Fast alle Fische sind tot.

Kurze Zeit später erhalten die Nachbarn und **Eigentümer** des Schrebergartens einen Brief von Herrn Voigt. Im Brief steht, er, Herr Voigt möchte den Schrebergarten **am Wochenende benutzen**. Wenn er den Schrebergarten am Wochenende benutzen darf, dann würde er, für ganz viele **gesunde Fische** im Teich garantieren.

Zusammenfassung

Ein Mann besitzt einen kleinen Garten mit einer Hütte, einen sogenannten Schrebergarten. Als einige Fische in seinem Teich sterben, verschenkt er den Schrebergarten an einen Nachbarn. Der Schrebergarten blüht, es leben viele Fische im Teich. Der Mann tötet viele Fische, und bietet den neuen Besitzer an, am Wochenende den Garten benutzen zu dürfen. Dafür würde er gesunde Fische garantieren.

Vokabeln und Redewendungen

Der Schrebergarten - *allotment*

Ausserhalb der grossen Städte - *outside of the larger cities*

eine kleine kleine Hütte - *a little hut*

diese Gärten und Hütten nennt man Schrebergarten - *these gardens and huts are called Schrebergarten*

die Eigentümer sind meistens Rentner - *The owners are mostly pensioners*

ab und zu - *sometimes* / once in a while

die Rentner freuen sich im Garten zu arbeiten - *the pensioners are glad to work in the garden*

ein kleiner Teich - *a little pond*

er kennt sich mit Fischen aus - *he knows about fish* j

jeden Fisch hat er einen Namen gegeben - he gave every fish its own name

Die Erklärung - *explanation*

er entscheidet - *he decides*

die Nachbarn - *the neighbors*

nach kurzer Zeit - *after a short time*

übernehmen - *to take over*

das Geschenk - *gift*

im hervorragenden Zustand - *in excellent condition*

die Eigentümer - *owner / proprietor*

blühen - *prosper*

sehr gepflegt - *well maintained*

gesunde Fische - *healthy fish*

Lernfragen

Warum hat Herr Voigt sich einen Schrebergarten gekauft?
Warum gibt Herr Voigt eine Anzeige auf?
Warum verschenkt Herr Voigt den Schrebergarten?

AUDIO (copy and paste into your browser)

http://bit.ly/2KtBNCO

Der Käse

Tim Peters hatte **sich verliebt.** Seit einigen Wochen hatte er eine neue Freundin. Seine neue Freundin war eine Frau, die **auf dem Markt arbeitete** und **nachmittag**s in die Bibliothek ging.

Herr Peters war seit einem Jahr Rentner. Er hatte viel **Freizeit**, und wenn er nicht in der Bibliothek Bücher las, ging er in die Geschäfte, hauptsächlich aus Langeweile. In der kleinen **Stadtbibliothek**, sass seit Wochen **eine Dame seines Alters** und las Bücher. Mit der Zeit kamen sie ins **Gespräch**.

Die Dame sagte, sie arbeitet morgens in einem **Käsegeschäft** auf dem Markt. Wenn der Markt nachmittags geschlossen war, ging sie zur **Erholung** in die Bibliothek. Beide hatten ein Hobby. Sie lasen beide klassische Literatur und **Kochbücher**. Herr Peters **besuchte sie** nie auf dem Markt, aber nach einigen Stunden in der Bibliothek gingen sie manchmal einen Kaffee trinken.

Eines Tages lud Herr Peters die Dame zu sich nach Hause ein.
Er wollte für sie kochen. Herr Peters war ein guter Hobbykoch. Sie trafen sich mehrmals bei Herrn Peters und nach einigen Wochen wurden sie schließlich **ein Paar.**

Allerdings war **die Beziehung** nicht ohne Probleme. Herr Peters mochte den **Geruch** der Dame nicht. **Er sagte ihr ganz offen, dass sie nach Käse riecht.** Deshalb mochte er sie auch nicht mehr nach Hause einladen. Herr Peters glaubte, jedes Mal nachdem die Dame ihn besucht hatte, roch sein **Schlafzimmer** nach Käse.

Als eines Tages Herr Peters ihr wieder sagte, sie rieche nach Käse, **wurde sie böse**. Sie sagte ihm, sie arbeitet in Wirklichkeit nicht auf dem Markt. Sie sagte, sie sei **in Wirklichkeit arbeitslos**. Herr Peters sagte, in Wirklichkeit ist er auch kein Rentner.

"Aber was ist denn dein wirklicher Beruf", fragte Herr Peters die Dame. "**Ich mache Fussmassagen**", sagte sie.
"Und was machst du, wenn du nicht in der Bibliothek bist", wollte die Dame wissen.
"**Ich arbeite auf dem Bauernhof im Schweinestall**. Aber zum Glück nur morgens".

Zusammenfassung

Ein älteres Paar haben sich in der Bibliothek kennengelernt. Die Frau sagt, sie verkauft Käse, der Mann sagt, er ist Rentner. Der Mann beschwert sich über ihren Geruch, weil er glaubt, das kommt vom Käse. Sie streiten sich. Am Ende erzählen sie sich ihren wirklichen Beruf.

Vokabeln und Redewendungen

sich verlieben - *to fall in love*
auf dem Markt arbeiten - *to work at the market*
nachmittags - *afternoon*
die Freizeit - *spare time / free time*
die Stadtbibliothek - *municipal library*
eine Dame seines Alters - *lady /woman of his age* das Gespräch - *conversation*
ein Käsegeschäft - *a cheese shop*
Erholung - *recreation*
Kochbücher - *cooking books*
besuchte sie - *visited her*
ein Paar - *couple*
die Beziehung - *relationship*
der Geruch - *smell*
das Schlafzimmer - *bedroom*
eines Tages lud Herr Meyer die Dame zu sich nach Hause ein - *One day Herr Meyer invited the lady to his house*
ich mache Fußmassagen - *I do foot massage*
ich arbeite auf dem Bauernhof im Schweinestall - *I work in a pig stall*

Lernfragen

Warum beschwert sich über ihren Geruch?

Was ist der wirkliche Beruf der Dame?

Was macht Herr Peters wenn er nicht in der Bibliothek ist?

AUDIO (copy and paste into your browser)

http://bit.ly/2G7NBFq

Ein besonderes Hobby

In Deutschland müssen alle Bürger **bei einer Behörde gemeldet** sein. Die erste Aufgabe der **Behörde** ist es, dass alle Daten der Bürger dort **gespeichtert** werden. Die Behörde darf die Daten auch **verkaufen. Die besten Klienten** sind häufig Rechtsanwälte.

Herr Meier ist **Rechtsanwalt**. In Deutschland gibt es Leute die illegale Musik oder Filme im Internet **runterladen**. Ein Rechtsanwalt kann **herausfinden,** wer das war. Dann bekommen die Leute einen Brief. Der Rechtsanwalt fordert Geld, oder er wird die Leute vor Gericht **verklagen. Dieser Brief hat einen Namen**. In Deutschland heisst so ein Brief **Abmahnung**.

Die meisten Leute zahlen den Rechtsanwalt. Herrn Meier sind die **Umstände der Fälle** egal. Herr Meier glaubt, er hat das Recht auf seiner Seite und Abmahnungen sind ein gutes Geschäft.

Herr Meier hat mit seinen Methoden Karriere gemacht. Mit der Zeit beschäftigt er mehrere Angestellte und kooperiert mit anderen Rechtsanwälten. Zusammen haben sie eine **Kanzlei** für Abmahnungen.

Die meisten Deutschen haben ein spezifisches Hobby. Herr Meier hat auch ein Hobby. **Er liebt Luxus Autos und Segelboote.** Auf Internet Forums schreibt Herr Meier Artikel über Luxus-Autos und Oldtimer. Sein letzter Artikel lautet: **Die Jagd** nach Luxus-Autos.

Eines Morgens kommt Herr Meier aus dem Haus und geht zu seinem Auto. Vor seinem Auto steht ein fremder Mann. In seiner Hand hält er eine **Stadtkarte**. Der Mann fragt Herrn Meier nach einer Straße. Herr Meier schaut auf die Karte.

Plötzlich zieht der Mann eine Pistole und schießt. **Der unbekannte Mann läuft davon**. Herr Meier wurde **erschossen**.

Später findet die Polizei ein Blatt Papier auf dem Fenster seines Autos. Auf dem Papier steht. "Mein Hobby die Abmahnmafia"

Zusammenfassung

Ein Rechtsanwalt schickt landesweit Briefe an Menschen, die angeblich illegal Musik aus dem Internet herunterladen. Die Briefe sind sogenannte Abmahnungen. Der Rechtsanwalt wird durch die Abmahnungen reich. Eines Tages wird zum Hobby eines Unbekannten.

Vokabeln und Redewendungen

bei einer Behörde gemeldet sein - *registered with a ministry*
Abmahnung - *a written warning*
speichern - *to safe*
verkaufen - *to sell*
die besten Klienten - *the best clients*

der Rechtsanwalt - *attorney at law / lawyer*
runterladen - *to download*
herausfinden - *to find out*
verklagen - *to sue*
dieser Brief hat einen Namen - *this letter has a name*
die Umstände der Fälle - *the circumstance of cases*
Herr Meier hat mit seinen Methoden Karriere gemacht –
Herr Meier had made a career of his methods
die Kanzlei - *joint business*
er liebt Luxusautos und Segelboote - *he loves luxury cars and sailing boats*
die Jagd - *the hunt*
der unbekannte Mann läuft davon - *the unknown man runs away*
er wurde erschossen - *he got shot*

Lernfragen

Warum ist Herrn Meier die Umstände der Fälle egal?
Welche Hobbys hat Herr Meier?
Warum, glaubst du, wird Herr Meier erschossen?

AUDIO (copy and paste into your browser)

http://bit.ly/2VEILps

Englisch im Ausland lernen

Die Eltern von Melanie **meinten es gut mit ihrer Tochter**. Sie wollten ihre Tochter als Aupair **nach England schicken**. Eine Agentur organisierte **die Unterbringung** bei einer englischen Familie. Der Grund, dass Melanie **mitmachen** sollte, war, ihr Englisch zu verbessern.

Die Agentur hatte **viel Geld verlangt.** Aber die Eltern von Melanie zahlten die Reise gerne, denn **die Ausbildung der Tochter war das Wichtigste**! Die Reise war schon lange geplant, und Melanie freute sich schon sehr. Ihre Eltern sprachen kein Englisch und wollten, dass Melanie perfektes Englisch lernt.

Die Gastfamilie war eine Familie, wo Melanie für einige Wochen wohnen sollte. Im **Vertrag** mit der Agentur stand auch, dass sie andere Aupair Mädchen treffen würde. Im August war es soweit. **Die Eltern begleiteten Melanie bis zum Flughafen**. Weinend **verabschiedeten** sich die Eltern von ihrer Tochter.

Einen Monat verblieb Melanie bei der fremden Familie. Sie durfte nicht telefonieren und im Haus gab es kein Internet. Deshalb ging Melanie oft **zur Post**, um ihren Eltern eine Postkarte zu schicken. Die Eltern waren sehr besorgt. Nur ein Brief erreichte die Eltern, **bevor Melanie zurück nach Deutschland flog**. Die Eltern freuten sich sehr ihre Tochter wiederzusehen. Natürlich wollten die Eltern wissen, **ob Melanie jetzt gut Englisch sprach**.

Die Tochter erklärte es ihnen. "Nein, Englisch habe ich nicht gelernt. Die Gastfamilie hat mehr Hindu als Englisch gesprochen. Das waren Einwanderer aus Indien."
"Das heißt, die ganze Reise war umsonst", fragte die Mutter.
"Nein **überhaupt nicht**", antwortete die Tochter. Aber ich weiß jetzt was Masala Fisch ist."

Zusammenfassung

Ein junges Mädchen wird von ihren Eltern nach England geschickt, um dort bei einer Familie als Aupair zu arbeiten und Englisch zu lernen. Als sie zurückkommt, hat sie kein Wort Englisch gelernt, aber indische Kochgerichte kennengelernt. Die Gastfamilie sind Einwanderer aus Indien.

Vokabeln und Redewendungen

meinten es gut mit ihrer Tochter - *meant well for their daughter*
nach England schicken - *to send to England*
die Unterbringung - *accommodation*
viel Geld verlangt - *demanded a lot of money*
die Ausbildung der Tochter war das Wichtigste – *the education of the daughter was most important*
die Gastfamilie - *host family*
der Vertrag - *the contract*
die Eltern begleiteten Melanie bis zum Flughafen – *the parents accompanied her to their airport*
verabschieden - *saying goodbye*
bevor Melanie zurück nach Deutschland flog – *before Melanie went back to Germany*
ob Melanie jetzt gut Englisch sprach - *if Melanie spoke English by now*
überhaupt nicht - *not at all*

Lernfragen

Warum schicken die Eltern Melanie nach England?
Warum lernt Melanie in England kein Englisch?
Was hat Melanie in England kennengelernt?

AUDIO (copy and paste into your browser)

http://bit.ly/2GgoEsx

Der Kunstkenner

Früher war Werner Mueller Schauspieler im Theater. In Berlin war er **relativ bekannt,** er hatte es sogar geschafft eine **wichtige Rolle für eine Fernsehserie** zu bekommen, wo er einen **glaubwürdigen** Kriminellen spielte. Herr Mueller war angeblich nie **unvermögend** und hatte sich schon immer für **Kunst und Antiquitäten** interessiert.

Jetzt war er über fünfzig, und die Rollen beim Film und Theater wurden weniger. Allerdings hatte sich Herr Mueller schon in **seiner Zeit als Schauspieler** auch einen Namen als Künstler für **Gemälde** gemacht. Man kann sagen, Herr Mueller war ein richtiger **Künstler** und auch Kunstliebhaber, denn er hatte ein grosses **Fachwissen**, insbesondere für antike Gemälde. Mit Impressionisten des 19. Jahrhunderts kannte er sich gut aus. Nach all den Jahren als Künstler, Schauspieler und Experte für Gemälden, war Herr Mueller auch in den Antiquitäten Geschäften und Galerien **ein gern gesehener Mann.** Herr Mueller kaufte viele Gemälde und Antiquitäten in den **Geschäften und Kunstgalerien**. Aber noch grösser war sein Ruf als guter **Einlieferer**. Die Qualität seiner Gemälde und **Ware**, die er zum Verkauf anbot, war erstklassig. Eines Tages konnte man in der Zeitung lesen, dass der bekannte Kunsthändler und Schauspieler Werner Mueller gestorben war.

Keiner wusste, woran er starb. Herr Mueller hatte keine Verwandte, deshalb suchten die Journalisten nach Freunden und Verwandten. **Vor kurzer Zeit wurden die Journalisten**

fündig. Herr Mueller war **ein entfernter Verwandter** von Hermann Goering.

Zusammenfassung

Ein Schauspieler sammelt Kunst und Antiquitäten. Er ist sehr beliebt, und liefert viel Ware in Geschäfte und Auktionshäuser ein. Nach dem Tod des Mannes, stellt sich heraus, dass er ein Verwandter Hermann Görings war.

Vokabeln und Redewendungen

relativ bekannt - *relatively known*
wichtige Rolle für eine Fernsehserie - *important role in a TV series*
glaubwürdig - *authentic*
guter Einlieferer - *good client*
unvermögend - *unfunded*
Kunst und Antiquitäten - *art and antiquities*
seine Zeit als Schauspieler - *his time as an actor*
das Gemälde - *painting*
der Künstler - *artist*
das Fachwissen - *expert knowledge*
Geschäften und Kunstgalerien - *business and art galleries*
die Ware - *merchandise*
keiner wusste, woran er starb - *nobody knew the reason for his death*
ein entfernter Verwandter - *a distant relative*

Lernfragen

Warum ist Herr Mueller so beliebt?

Woher, glaubst du, hat Herr Mueller die Ware bekommen?

Was konnte man eines Tages in der Zeitung lesen?

AUDIO (copy and paste into your browser)

http://bit.ly/2G6Ugj0

Gastronomen

Die zwei Brüder Anton und Tim sind **gelernte Gastronomen**, ausgebildet an einer **Fachschule** in der Schweiz. Beide habe schon in bekannten französischen Restaurants gearbeitet und sich **einen guten Ruf erworben.**

Vor zehn Jahren eröffneten sie ihr eigenes Restaurant in Berlin. Es **dauerte** nur wenige Jahre, bis das Restaurant **tatsächlich** mit dem ersten Michelin Star ausgezeichnet wurde. Finanziell wurde das Restaurant zum großen **Erfolg** und **ein zweiter Stern folgte nur zwei Jahre später.**

Letztes Jahr eröffneten die Brüder ein zweites Restaurant in einen anderen **Stadtteil.** Dann kam der grosse Schock. Eines Tages, erfuhren die Brüder, dass sie nur noch **einen Michelin Star für das erste Restaurant** erhielten. Ein Freund, der für einen **Verlag** arbeitet, verriet den Brüdern, dass sie einen Stern weniger bekamen, **weil sie ihre Suppe in Plastikbeutel** von einem Restaurant zum anderen trugen. Die Brüder waren **sehr verärgert**. In einer lokalen Radioshow beschwerten sich die Brüder über **die Bewerter.**

Danach folgten viele Anrufe. **Der Grund der Anrufe war eine Überraschung.** Viele Kunden riefen im Restaurant an und wollten **Suppe zum Mitnehmen** kaufen. Es folgten immer mehr tägliche **Anfragen** nach Suppen.

Durch die Radioshow kamen immer **mehr Gäste. Jeden Abend** wurde mehr Suppe zum Mitnehmen verkauft. **Der Umsatz stieg** enorm.

Schließlich planten die Brüder ein drittes Restaurant. Diesmal Suppen mit Lieferservice

Zusammenfassung

Zwei Brüder haben mehrere Restaurant. eröffnet. Sie haben bereits zwei Michelin Sterne. Weil sie die Suppen in Plastikbeutel von einem Restaurant zum anderen transportieren, wird ihnen ein Stern abgezogen. Viele Gäste erfahren davon und kaufen Suppe zum Mitnehmen.

Vokabeln und Redewendungen

gelernte Gastronomen - *professional restaurateurs / gastronoms*
die Fachschule - *technical college / specialized school*
einen guten Ruf erworben - *gain a good reputation*
vor zehn Jahren eröffneten sie ihr eigenes Restaurant –
ten years ago they opened their own restaurant
es dauert - *it lasts*
tatsächlich - *actually*
der Erfolg - *success*
einen Michelin Stern für das erste Restaurant –
a Michelin star for the first restaurant
der Verlag - *publisher*
ihre Suppe in Plastikbeutel - *their soup in plastic bags*

sehr verärgert - *very annoyed*
die Bewerter - *the reviewers*
der Grund der Anrufe war eine Überraschung - *the reason for the calls were a surprise*
eine Suppe zum mitnehmen - *a soup for to go*
mehr Anfragen - *more requests*
jeden Abend - *every evening*
der Umsatz stieg - *the revenues increased*
Schließlich planten die Brüder ein drittes Restaurant –
Finally the brothers made plans for a third restaurant

AUDIO (copy and paste into your browser)

http://bit.ly/2UNvBt7

Das Handtuch

Herr Tamm ist ein **Geschäftsmann**. Er besitzt einen kleinen **Imbiss**, dort verkauft er meistens frittierte Schnitzel und **Pommes**.

Mr. Tamm is a businessman. He owns a small restaurant where he mostly sells schnitzel and fries.

Er hat viele **Stammgäste** und die meisten Gäste **mögen** seine Gerichte.

Nach **Feierabend** besucht er **häufig** in eine Sauna um sich zu entspannen.

He has a lot of regular customers and most of the customers like his food.

In the after-work hours he frequently visits a sauna to calm down and relax

Vor kurzer Zeit ging Herr Tamm wieder in die Sauna. **Eigentlich** ist es eine Sauna Landschaft, wie man sie häufig in Deutschland findet. Sie sind **eingerichtet** mit Saunen und Schwimmbad.

A little time ago Mr. Tamm went again to the sauna. Actually it is typical Sauna facility as they can be found a lot in Germany . They are furnished with saunas and a swimming pool.

An diesem Abend schien die Temperatur in der Sauna **besonders** hoch. Herr Tamm saß schon auf der Bank als die Tür aufging. Ein Mann kam herein. Herr Tamm **erkannte** den Mann sofort. Er war ein bekannter **Kunde**. Allerdings hatte der Kunde ihn vormals **denunziert**, weil der Kunde glaubte, der Imbiss sei **dreckig**.

That day the temperature of the sauna seemed to be especially high. Mr. Tamm was already on the bench when the door opened. A man came in. Mr. Tamm recognized the man immediately. It was a known customer. However, once the customer had denounced him because he thought the restaurant was dirty.

Auch der andere Mann erkannte Herrn Tamm.

Der Kunde lächelte: "Guten Abend Herr Tamm, wie geht es Ihnen?"

"**Alles in Ordnung**, vielen Dank."

"Schwitzen reinigt die Haut", sagte der Mann.

The other man also recognized Mr. Tamm.

The client smiled: "Good evening, Mr. Tamm, how are you?"

"All fine, thank you."

"Sweating cleans the skin", said the man.

Herr Tamm hatte genug und verließ die Sauna. Er ging zum **duschen**. Diesmal duschte Herr Tamm lange, denn er hatte sich über den Mann geärgerte . Nach dem duschen ging Herr Tamm in die **Umkleidekabine**. Einen großen Saal mit vielen Schränken.

Mr. Tamm had enough and left the sauna. He went to shower. This time Mr. Tamm took a long shower, because he got annoyed by the man. After the shower Mr. Tamm went into the changing room. A big room with lots of closets.

Alle **Handtücher** hingen an einem Haken. Herr Tamm trocknete sich ab. Aber das Handtuch war nass, trotzdem fühlte Herr Tamm sich jetzt besser. Draußen vor dem Ausgang, traf Herr Tamm den Kunde wieder.

All the towels were hanging on a hook. Mr. Tamm toweled himself. But the towel was wet, anyway Mr. Tamm felt better now. Outside in front of the exit, Mr. Tamm met the client again.

Der Mann schaute Herrn Tamm an und lächelte: "Entschuldigen Sie, Herr Tamm, aber sie haben mein Handtuch **benutzt und mitgenommen.**"

Herr Tamm schüttele den Kopf: "Das glaube ich nicht."

"Schauen Sie doch bitte in ihre Tasche", sagte der Mann.

Herr Tamm öffnete seine Tasche und zog das nasse Handtuch heraus.

The man looked at Mr. Tamm and smiled: "Excuse me, Mr. Tamm, but you have used and taken my towel!"

Mr. Meier shook his head. "No, I don't think so."

"Please have a look in your bag." said the man.

Mr. Meier opened his bag and pulled the towel out.

Der andere Mann lächelte. "Sehen Sie hier. Dort **in der Ecke** des Handtuches sehen Sie meine Buchstaben, markiert mit schwarzer Schrift."

"A.H.", fragte Herr Tamm.

"Das bin ich".

Herr Tamm gab dem Mann sein Handtuch zurück. Danach ging er nie wieder die Sauna besuchen.

The other man still smiled. "Look here. There in the corner of the towel you see my letters, marked with a black marker.

"A.H." asked Mr. Meier.

"That's me." said the man.

Mr. Meier gave the towel back to the man. Afterwards he never went back to the sauna again.

Zusammenfassung

Herr Tamm besucht eine Sauna um zu relaxen. In der Sauna trifft er einen Kunden. Herr Tamm mag den Kunden nicht, denn dieser hatte ihn vormals denunziert. Unbewusst trocknet sich Herr Tamm mit dem Handtuch des Kunden ab und nimmt es mit. Am Ausgang wird Herr Tamm vom Kunden abgefangen und befragt.

Vokabeln

der Geschäftsmann - *businessman*

der Imbiss - *small restaurant*

die Pommes - *chips / fries*

die Stammgäste - *regular guests*

mögen - *to like something*

der Feierabend - *after-work hours*

häufig - *frequent / frequently*

eigentlich - *actually*

eingerichtet - *furnished*

denunziert/ denunzieren - *to denounce someone*

besonders - *especially*

erkannte (erkennen) - *recognized*

ein Kunde - *a customer*

dreckig - *dirty*

alles in Ordnung - *everything is okay*

duschen - *to shower*

die Handtücher - *towels*

draußen - *outside*

in der Ecke - *in the corner*

benutzt und mitgenommen - *used and took it*

Beantworte die folgenden Fragen im Auswahlverfahren.

1. Was für eine Art Geschäft hat Herr Tamm?
a) Ein Theater
b) Er verkauft Handys
c) Er verkauft Puppen
d) Er hat einen Imbiss

2. Was macht Herr Tamm häufig nach Feierabend?
a) Er geht in eine Sauna
b) Er geht ins Theater
c) Er besucht eine Freundin
d) Er geht zum Essen

3. Warum hat der Kunde Herrn Tamm denunziert?
a) Der Kunde mochte das Essen nicht
b) Der Kunde fand, der Imbiss sei dreckig
c) Herr Tamm schwitzt immer in der Sauna
d) Der Kunde findet Herrn Tamm dreckig

4. Nach der Sauna beschuldigt der Kunde Herrn Meier:
a) Herr Tamm hat in der Sauna zu sehr geschwitzt
b) Herr Tamm hat nicht "Guten Morgen" gesagt
c) Herr Tamm hat sein Handtuch benutzt
d) Herr Tamm hat nicht geduscht

Lösung aus Kurzgeschichte 1
1d 2a 3b 4c

AUDIO (copy and paste into your browser)

http://bit.ly/2USnNq7

AEL
ASSOCIATION OF
EUROPEAN LANGUAGES
Language
Starter
Book
Academy Der Sprachclub
GERMAN
Phrase Book
Your Practical German
Phrasebook For Travelers Of
Germany Students And Kids
Over 800 Realistic German Phrases,
Terms And Expressions Used By
Native German Speakers

German Phrase Book

Your Practical German Phrasebook for Travelers of Germany Students and Kids

Over 800 Realistic German Phrases Terms And Expressions

Used by Native German Speakers

Contents

Phrases for Travelers

Airport and Flights

Taxi and Hiring a Car

Driving and Parking

Renting a Car and Car Trouble

Transportation Phrases

In the House, Friends and Guests

Guests and Invitations

Cleaning

Household Chores

Business, Renting and Real Estate

Business and Negotiations

Banking Phrases and Terms

Insurance -- Phrases and Terms

Real Estate – Phrases and Terms

Legal Terms and Situations

Education, At Work and Sports

Education and University

At Work

Sports

Small Talk and Entertainment

Talk About Yourself

Trivial Conversation Phrases for Travelers

Entertainment and Recreation

Orders

Holidays, Seasons, Christmas

Seasons and Festivals
Public Holidays and Terms for Vacations
Christmas Phrases
Church and Religion
Signs and Notices
Social Media, Computer and Hobbies
Social Media, IT and Computer
Arts & Hobbies
Words and Phrases for Kids Made Easy

Pronunciation

German Words - Spelling and Pronunciation

German spelling and pronunciation isn't as troublesome as one might think, because most vowels and consonants are related to the English language. You basically spell exactly what you hear, and once you get used and understand the sounds of German letters, it becomes easy and fast to spell the language. However, it is important to learn how to pronounce the words clearly and correctly so you can understand at once what is said when someone speaks to you in German.

Learning the proper pronunciation starts by actively practicing the pronunciation of letters. Once you have learned how specific letters or combinations of letters are pronounced, you should be able to speak with confidence and say almost all words correctly.

The Alphabet - Consonants and Vowels

The German language uses the 26 - letter Latin alphabet which is also used in English, but in German each letter either has a different name is unique or is pronounced differently. German also has four additional distinct letter sounds which will be explained by practical examples. Some letters may be challenging to English speakers as there is no parallel sound in English.

Before we get into learning the consonants and vowels let's take a quick glance at this overview of the alphabet and pronunciation:

A (a) /ɑ:/Long 'a' as 'a' in 'father' (ah).

B (be) /be:/ Pronounced like 'p' when at the end of a word

C (ce) /tse:/ See combination letter forms; without a following 'h': before 'e', 'i', 'y', 'ä', 'ö' like the German letter 'z' else like 'k'

D (de) /de:/ Pronounced like 't' when at the end of a word; slightly more "dental"

E (e) /e:/ Long 'e' as 'a' in 'late' (ay) without (!) the (y). Short 'e' as 'e' in 'pet'. In "unstressed" syllables like 'a' in 'about' or 'e' in 'garden'

F (ef) /ɛf/

G (ge) /geː/ Pronounced like 'g' in 'get'; pronounced like 'k' when at the end of a word; pronounced like 'ich'-sound (see below) in the suffix '-ig' at the end of words

H (ha) /hɑː/ like 'h' in house, only at the beginning of words or a syllable before 'a', 'i', 'o', 'u', 'y', 'ä', 'ö', 'ü' (only if these vowels don't belong to a suffix), else silent

I (i) /iː/ Long 'i' as 'e' in 'seen' (ee); short 'i' as 'i' in 'pit'

J (jot) /jot/ Pronounced like 'y' in 'yard'

K (ka) /kɑː/

L (el) /ɛl/ Slightly more "dental"

M (em) /ɛm/

N (en) /ɛn/ Slightly more "dental"; before 'a', 'i', 'o', 'u', 'y', 'ä', 'ö', 'ü' (only if these vowels don't belong to a suffix)

O (o) /oː/ Long 'o' as 'o' in 'open' (oh), there is no movement in the sound as in the English equivalent. Short 'o' as 'o' in 'pot'

P (pe) /peː/

Q (ku) /kuː/ Pronounced like 'k'; only occurs in the combination 'qu', which is pronounced like 'kv' not like 'kw'

R (er) /ɛʀ/ trilled with the front or back of the tongue, depending on area (see below)

S (es) /ɛs/ In Germany, pronounced like the English 'z'; pronounced like 's' in 'sound' when at the end of a word, after consonants (except 'l', 'm', 'n', ng') and before consonants; in Austria, pronounced like 'z' only when it appears between two vowels, pronounced like 's' otherwise. Pronounced like 'sh' in the beginning of a word before 'p' or 't'

T (te) /teː/ Slightly more "dental"

U (u) /uː/ Long 'u' as 'oo' in 'moon' (oo); short 'u' as 'u' in 'put'

V (vau) /faʊ/ Pronounced like 'f' when at the end of a word, in the prefixes 'ver-' and 'vor-' and in a few, but often used words -in most cases of Germanic origin-, in general at the beginning of German family and geographical names. In all other cases like 'v'

W (ve) /veː/ Pronounced like 'v'

X (iks) /ɪks/ Pronounced like 'ks'

Y (üpsilon) /ʏpsɪlon/ Pronounced like 'ü' (see below), except in words of English origin, where it is pronounced like in English

Z (zet) /tsɛt/ Pronounced like 'ts'

Pronouncing “Umlaute” and Vowels

Our Tips for Pronouncing "Umlaute"

ä, ö, and ü

To pronounce the "ä"sound, say “ay” as in *May* or as in the German word crow : *die Krähe*.

While continuing to spell this sound just tightly round your lips. Look in a mirror and make sure your lips are actually rounded. *Bitte sehr!* The resulting sound is the : **ä** sound. (sounds like to *bed*)

A similar method can be used with the **ü**-sound. The **ü** sound doesn't have a equal in English. Again, while saying the sound, try to round your lips. Then the resulting sound is the **ü**-sound. In case you know how to pronounce **u** in French, it sounds just like the German **ü**

Like any unfamiliar sounds, being able to pronounce the German **ö** and **ü** correctly, can only come with repeated practice!

More About Vowels

Now let's take a look at German vowels. To a non-German speaker German vowels probably sound strange and very different, so it is worth studying and practicing them, especially if your native tongue is other than English.

In German there are eight vowels: *a, e, i, o, u,* plus the "mutated vowels", the so-called *Umlaute: ä, ö,* and *ü.*

German vowels and Umlaute are all pronounced in a pure and strong way, and unlike in English and most other Germanic languages where vowels tend to be pronounced softer and often as diphthongs.

Also, there is a difference in length.

Vowels can be long or short. When a vowel is followed by a double consonant, for example like double "l" or double "m" they are short, but when a vowel is followed by only one consonant, the following words are using long vowels:

schnell (short) - quick
haben (long) – to have
der Schnee (long) - snow
hell (short) – bright
der Regen (long) – rain

/i/ like in "with" (short) or "feet" (long)
Ich (short) – I

/o/ like in "hot" (short) or "door" (long) *offen* (short) – open
der Ofen (long) – oven/stove

/u/ like in "bush" (short) or "boot" (long)
(ich) muss (short) – I must
der Kuchen (long) – cake

- **The German *Umlaute* are vowels and can be transcribed as follows:**

ä (a-Umlaut) – ae
ö (b-Umlaut) – oe
ü (u.Umlaut) – ue

Pronunciation: ä like in "head," but with a wide opened mouth

die Hände – hands
dier Äpfel - apples

Pronunciation: ö like in "burn, heard, sir"
öffnen – to open
die *Köpfe* – heads

Pronunciation: ü like in "Tyrell, new, few"
die Tür – door
über – over/above

You should know that there's a slight difference in open and closed pronunciation of the *Umaute ä, ö, ü*.

You might also notice that when trying to imitate the *Umlaute* there is a slight difference in the mouth position of your lips. German pronunciations are more harsh, from round closed to wide open.

However, this is something you can improve on and is relatively easy to do by carefully listening to the pronunciations and by imitating those sounds.

- **The German *Umlaute* are vowels and can be transcribed as follows:**

ä – ae
ö – oe
ü – ue

/ä/ like in "head," but with a wide opened mouth

die Hände – hands
dier Äpfel - apples

/ö/ like in "burn, heard, sir" *öffnen* – to open
die *Köpfe* – heads

/ü/ like in "Tyrell, new, few" *die Tür* – door

über – over/above

- You also have to know that there is a slight difference in open and closed pronunciation of the "Umaute" sounds *ä, ö, ü*. Again, this is something you can improve on, because once you know the basic sounds and pronunciations of the vowels and by listening carefully to the German pronunciation, it will become easier. You should also try to imitate those sounds. You will probably notice that there is a slight difference in the mouth position of your lips. German pronunciations are generally more harsh, the libs are formed more round and at times the mouth is used more wide open.

Pronouncing Diphthongs and Cognates

Diphthongs are combinations that consist of at least two vowels in one syllable.

But instead of being pronounced separately, (or in two separate words) the two letters have actually one sound or pronunciation. A typical example would be the au combination.

Our tip:

The diphthong *au* in German sounds like *OW* as in English “couch” , the "ou" being an English diphthong; the *au* is also part of some German words such as *lauschen,* or *autsch*, which is pronounced almost the same as “couch” in English!)

ai

Pronunciation: Like the vowel sound in English "mine", but more tense and clipped.

oi

Pronunciation: Like the vowel sound in English "coin", but more short, tense, and clipped.

au

Pronunciation: Like the vowel sound in English "house", but slightly more tense and clipped.

Near Cognates

There are words in German which bear almost the same spelling as their English counterpart.

Here are some of the usual spelling conventions used in German: In most German words, the "c" in English becomes "k".

The "ou" in words like "trout" or "mouth" becomes "au" in German.

Only a few words in German end in "-ig". However "y" ending in adjectives like "watery" becomes "- ig" in German. The "y" ending in nouns like "story"becomes "-ie"in German.

-lich is fairly common in German which means "ly" ending in nouns like "family" becomes "-lich"in German.

The infamous and hard to pronounce"ch" is not as difficult as its reputation. It is pronounced like a soft c or soft k. For example, In the word "sechs" (six), the pronunciation is easy for English natives: "zeks". Every time you see "chs", it is pronounced like "ks" -it's one sound for us, but there are some exceptions like ". Buchregal" (because it's a compound of the words Buch and Regal)

Phrasebook

Greetings and Everyday Expressions

Formal and Informal Introductions

What's your name?
¿Wie heißt du / Wie heißen Sie?

To ask someone's name (formal)
What's your name?
Wie heißen Sie?

To ask someone's name (informal, friends)
What's your name?
Wie heißt du?

My name is (first and last name)_______.
Mein Name ist_______.

You can use any of these phrases to express your pleasure at a meeting:

I'm pleased to meet you! / Nice to meet you!
Es freut mich Sie kennenzulernen

Glad you came
Schön, dass Sie gekommen sind
Nett, dass Sie gekommen sind

It was a pleasure to meet you
Schön Sie getroffen zu haben

Nett Sie getroffen zu haben

To introduce people to each other, you can say:

This is my friend John
Das ist mein Freund John.

John, this is my sister Helga
John, das ist meine Schwester Helga

Polite Expressions

Thank you very much!
Vielen Dank!

All okay
Alles in Ordnung

No thanks
Nein danke

You are welcome
Keine Ursache / Gerne

Excuse me, please
Entschuldigen sie bitte

Sorry
Entschuldigung

I am sorry
Es tut mir leid

This is very kind
Das ist sehr nett

Phrases for Greeting Friends & Family

Good morning!
Guten Morgen
(For formal meetings, Germans say often "Guten Tag" -- good day)

Good evening
Guten Abend

How are you?
Wie geht es Ihnen? (formal)
Wie geht es dir? (informal, friends)

Very well, thank you.
Vielen Dank, sehr gut

See you later
Bis später

Until then
Bis dann

Good night
Gute Nacht

What's going on?
Was ist los?

What's happening?
Was ist passiert?

Let me introduce you to my mother
Ich stelle Ihnen/dir meine Mutter vor

Do you have siblings?
Haben Sie/Hast du Geschwister?

This is my brother
Das ist mein Bruder

This is my sister
Das ist meine Schwester

This is my uncle
Das ist meine Onkel

This is my aunt
Das ist meine Tante

This is my grandmother
Das ist meine Großmutter

This is my grandfather
Das ist meine Großvater

I have a son / I have a daughter
Ich habe einen Sohn / Ich habe eine Tochter

I am waiting for my mother
Ich warte auf meine Mutter

When can we meet?
Wann können wir uns treffen?

Where can we meet?
Wo können wir uns treffen?

This person is part of my family
Diese Person gehört zu meiner Familie

I have a boyfriend / a girlfriend
Ich habe einen Freund/eine Freundin

I invite you to meet my family
Ich lade dich ein, meine Familie kennenzulernen

Visit me at home
Besuche mich zu Hause

Common Everyday German Phrases

I want, I don’t want
Ich möchte / Ich möchte nicht

I would like..
Ich würde gerne...

Where is..?
Wo ist..?

How much does it cost?
Wieviel kostet das?

What time is it?
Wie spät ist es?

Do you have...?
Haben Sie…?

I have / I don't have...
Ich habe / Ich habe kein..

I understand / I don't understand
Ich verstehe / Ich verstehe nicht

Do you understand?
Verstehen Sie? / Verstehst du?

Help and Health Issues

Asking Directions

Where is..?
Wo ist.. ?

Can you tell me the way to..?
Können Sie mir die Richtung nach...zeigen ?

Can you show me on the map?
Können Sie es mir auf der Karte zeigen?

Can you walk?
Kannst du gehen?

Where are the toilets?
Wo sind die Toiletten?

Is it near?
Ist es nahe?

Is it far?
Ist es weit?

Is there a bus?
Gibt es einen Bus?

Where does this road go to?
Wohin führt die Strasse?

Which direction?
Welche Richtung?

I am looking for the next exit
Ich suche die nächste Ausfahrt

Is this the street to...?
Ist das die Strasse nach..?

Where can I find the....?
Wo finde ich ...?

Left
Links

Right
Rechts

Turn right
Geradeaus

On the corner
An der Ecke

Opposite the gas / petrol station
Gegenüber der Tankstelle

You have to go back
Sie müssen zurück

Keep going straight ahead
Weiter geradeaus

Take the road to...
Nehme sie die Strasse nach...

Under the bridge
Unter der Brücke

At the crossroads
An der Kreuzung

You go as far as..
Sie gehen bis..

….next to the supermarket
...neben dem Supermarkt

Cross the street
Die Kreuzung überqueren

On the second floor
Im zweiten Stock

The supermarket is in front of the church.
Der Supermarkt befindet sich vor der Kirche

The embassy is across the street.
Die Botschaft befindet sich gegenüber der Strasse

The hospital is around the corner
Das Krankenhaus ist um die Ecke

About how long will it take?
Wie lange dauert das?

You go straight, and then you turn left.
Sie gehen geradeaus, dann gehen Sie links

Medical Issues and Emergencies

Where is the next hospital?
Wo ist das nächste Krankenhaus?

Our insurance in the US will pay for this
Unsere Versicherung zahlt das

My wife needs surgery
Meine Frau muss operiert usti

I need to have my tooth fixed
Mein Zahn muss behandelt werden

Do you have painkillers?
Haben Sie Schmerztabletten?

I am allergic against... (fish) --
Ich bin gegen (Fisch) allergisch

I had an accident; send an ambulance
Ich habe einen Unfall gehabt; schicken Sie einen Krankenwagen

I need a remedy against headache--
Ich brauche ein Mittel gegen Schmerzen

I cut myself; do you have a bandage?
Ich habe mich geschnitten; haben sie ein Pflaster?

Can you send a doctor to my house?
Können Sie uns einen Arzt nach Hause schicken?

Crime and Help Phrases

I need a doctor
Ich brauche einen Arzt

I need help!
Ich brauche Hilfe!

Call the police!
Ruf die Polizei!

I am going to call the police
Ich werde die Polizei rufen

This is an emergency
Das ist ein Notfall

Stop the thief!
Haltet den Dieb!

I am the witness
Ich bin der Zeuge

I have not seen anything
Ich habe nichts gesehen

I have been robbed
Ich wurde überfallen

I have been attacked
Ich wurde angegriffen

They broke into my apartment
Man hat in meine Wohnung eingebrochen

They stole my wallet
Man hat meine Brieftasche gestohlen

I have a complaint
Ich habe eine Beschwerde

I want to file a police report
Ich möchte eine Anzeige aufgeben

I need to contact my embassy
Ich muss mit meiner Botschaft sprechen

I want to speak with a lawyer
Ich will mit einem Rechtsanwalt sprechen

I lost my money
Ich habe mein Geld verloren

I forgot my passport
Ich habe meinen Reisepass vergessen

I left the keys in the room
Ich habe die Schlüssel im Zimmer gelassen

I have to leave now!
Ich muss jetzt los!

General Repairs

This is damaged
Das ist beschädigt

We need tools
Wir brauchen Werkzeug

Can you repair it?
Kannst du es reparieren?

Can you do it quickly?
Können Sie es schnell machen?

What's the problem?
Was ist das Problem?

Is it broken?
Ist es kaputt

Can you glue it?
Kann man es kleben?

Here is the guarantee
Hier ist die Garantie

Can you take a look at it?
Darf ich es mir anschauen?

We need help
Wir brauchen Hilfe

We need a specialist
Wir brauchen einen Spezialisten

We need a replacement
Wir brauchen Ersatz

I need nails and a hammer
Ich brauche Nägel und einen Hammer

I need a saw
Wir brauchen eine Sage

Who can fix it?
Wer kann das heil machen?

Accommodations, Restaurants and Shopping

Accommodations

Wie have a reservation.
Wir haben eine Reservierung.

We need a large room
Wir brauchen ein großes Zimmer.

When can we check in?
Wann dürfen wir einchecken?

At what time do we have to check out?
Um wieviel Uhr müssen wir auschecken?

We'd like to have a room with twin beds.
Wir möchten ein Zimmer mit zwei Betten.

We like to have a quiet room.
Wir möchten ein ruhiges Zimmer.

Do we have to pay now?
Müssen wir sofort bezahlen?

Is breakfast included?
Ist Frühstück inklusive?

Can we get breakfast delivered to the room?
Können wir das Frühstück aufs Zimmer bekommen?

Does this room have aircondition?
Hat das Zimmer eine Klimaanlage?

Do you have a city map?
Haben Sie einen Stadtplan?

Can we leave our suitcases here?
Können wir unsere Koffer hierlassen?

Can someone help us with the suitcases?
Kann uns jemand mit den Koffern helfen?

We'd like to cancel our booking.
Wir möchten unsere Buchung stornieren.

Restaurants and Eating Out

I like to order a coffee
Ich möchte einen Kaffee bestellen

Can I have the menu please?
Darf ich bitte die Karte sehen?

We would like to reserve a table
Wir möchten einen Tisch reservieren

Do you have vegetarian meals?
Haben Sie vegetarische Gerichte?

I like to have my steak medium
Ich mag das Steak medium

The food is unacceptable
Das Essen ist nicht akzeptierbar

Bring me something else
Bringen Sie mir etwas anderes

I would like to order a glass of white wine
Ich möchte ein Glas Weisswein bestellen

The bill / check please
Die Rechnung bitte

The tip is not included
Das Trinkgeld ist nicht enthalten

Foods and Restaurants

What is your favorite food?
Was ist dein/Ihr Lieblingsessen?

Can you please say what that is?
Können patter bitte sagen was das ist?

The taste is very interesting
Es schmeckt sehr interessant

This is very delicious
Das ist sehr lecker

We would like to order..
Wir möchten bestellen

Can you bring us a larger portion please?
Können Sie uns bitte eine grössere Portion bringen?

What are the ingredients for this dish?
Was sind die Zutaten für dieses Gericht?

How do you make stew?
Wie macht man Eintopf?

We eat traditional food
Wir essen traditionelles Essen

We are on a diet
Wir sind auf Diät

How many calories are in there?
Wie viele Kalorien sind dort drin?

What food do you recommend?
Welches Essen empfehlen Sie? /empfiehlst du?

What German dishes do you know?
Welches deutsches Gericht kennen Sie?

What are typical German ingredients?
Was sind typische deutsche Zutaten?

First fry it then you bake it
Zuerst frittieren, danach backen

We prefer a strong flavor
Wir bevorzugen einen starken Geschmack

We cook at home
Wir kochen zu Hause

How do you cook this dish?
Wie kocht man dieses Gericht?

We are looking for a supermarket
Wir suchen einen Supermarkt

Shopping and Renting

We are looking for a good souvenir
Wir suchen ein gutes Souvenir

Do you have a larger size? This is too small
Haben Sie eine Nummer größer? Das ist zu klein

This shirt is too expensive
Das Hemd ist zu teuer

Is the price negotiable?
Ist der Preis verhandelbar?

I only want to buy fresh ingredients
Ich möchte nur frische Zutaten

How much is the weekly rent?
Wieviel kostet die Wochenmiete?

Do we have to pay a deposit?
Müssen wir eine Kaution zahlen?

We are looking for a furnished room
Wir suchen ein möbliertes Zimmer

We like to rent this room by the month
Wir möchten das Zimmer für einen Monat mieten

When do I get my money back?
Wann bekomme ich mein Geld zurück?

The house needs to be cleaned
Das Haus muss gereinigt werden

Travel, Cars and Transportation

Phrases for Travelers

I am looking for a hotel
Ich suche ein Hotel

I need a room with a bathroom
Ich brauche ein Zimmer mit Bad

Do you have an inexpensive room?
Haben Sie ein günstiges Zimmer?

Can you call me a taxi, please?
Können Sie mir ein Taxi bestellen?

Bring me to the airport!
Bringen Sie mich zum Flughafen

When is the next flight to..?
Wann fliegt der nächste Flug nach...?

At what time does the flight from...arrive?
Um wieviel Uhr kommt der nächste Flug aus....?

Where is the exchange?
Wo gibt es ein Wechselbüro?

Where is the bank?
Wo befindet sich die Bank?

Where is the bus station? --
Wo ist der Busbahnhof?

Where can I buy a ticket to...?
Wo bekomme ich ein Ticket nach..?

I pay with my credit card
Ich zahle mit meiner Kredit Karte

Airport and Flights

What is our flight number?
Was ist unsere Flugnummer?

I have a reservation
Ich habe eine Reservierung

Have only one suitcase
Ich habe nur einen Koffer

I have only hand luggage
Ich habe nur Handgepäck

Can we take that into the cabin?
Können wir das in die Kabine nehmen?

Do I need a visa?
Brauche ich ein Visum?

Where do I claim the luggage?
Wo kann ich das Gepäck abholen?

Where can we find gate number.. ?
Wo finden wir Gate / Flugsteig Nummer.. ?

I need to change my ticket
I muss meine Flugkartet wechseln

The airline changed our flight
Die Fluggesellschaft hat unser Ticket geändert

I would like to have a window seat
Ich möchte eine Fensterplatz

I would like to have an aisle seat
Ich möchte einen Platz am Gang

Can I get an upgrade?
Kann ich ein(e) Upgrade / Aufwertung bekommen?

Do we have to go through security?
Müssen wir durch die Sicherheitskontrolle?

Where is the information desk?
Wo ist der Informationsschalter?

This computer belongs to me
Der Computer gehört mir

I have nothing to declare
Ich habe nichts zu verzollen

Do you know at what time are we arriving?
Wissen Sie wann wir ankommen?

I would like to change my seat
Ich möchte meinen Sitz wechseln

Where does this plane fly to?
Wohin fliegt dieses Flugzeug?

Where is the arrival terminal?
Wo ist der Ankunfts--Terminal?

Where is the terminal for departure?
Wo ist der Abflugs--Terminal?

Our suitcase has been stolen!
Unser Koffer wurde geklaut!

Do you have a hotel voucher?
Haben Sie einen Hotel Gutschein?

Where do I find the shuttle transfer to Terminal 1?
Wo finde ich den Shuttle Bus zum Terminal 1?

Where do I find the car rental companies?
Wo finde ich die Autovermietung?

Taxi and Hiring a Car

I want to hire a car
Ich möchte eine Auto mieten

I need it for one week
Ich brauche i emir Woche

Please explain the documents
Bitte erklären Sie die Dokumente

Must I return the car here?
Muss ich das Auto hier abgeben?

Is there a charge per i emirr?
Muss man pro Kilometer bezahlen

Please show me how to operate the car?
Können i emir zeigen, wie das Auto funktioniert

I would like to rent a small size car
Ich möchte ein kleineres Auto

Do you have a car with automatic?
Haben Sie ein Auto mit Automatik?

I want to leave the car at the airport
Ich will das Auto am Flughafen lassen

Where is the tool kit?
Wo sind die Werkzeuge?

We don't need additional insurance!

Wir brauchen keine Zusatz Versicherung!

What is the emergency number?
Was ist die Notfall Nummer?

Where can I get a taxi?
Wo kann ich ein Taxi bekommen?

Take me to the airport please
Bringen Sie mich bitte zum Flughafen

To the bus station please!
Zur Busstation bitte!

Take me to this address
Bringen Sie mich zu dieser Adresse

Why is it so expensive
Warum ist das so teuer?

I need help with the suitcase
Ich brauche Hilfe mit dem Koffer

Please don't interrupt our conversation
Bitte unterbrechen Sie unsere Konversation nicht

Turn off the music
Schalten Sie die Musik aus

Turn on the taximeter
Stellen Sie das Taximeter an

Driving and Parking

Is the traffic heavy?
Gibt es viel Verkehr?

Is there a different way to the airport?
Gibt es einen anderen Weg zum Flughafen?

What is causing this traffic jam?
Was verursacht den Stau?

What is the speed limit?
Wie ist die Höchstgeschwindigkeit?

Is there a toll on this motorway?
Gibt es Zoll auf der Strasse?

Can you clean the windscreen?
Können Sie die Windschutzscheibe reinigen?

We got lost
Wir haben uns verlaufen (walking)
Wir haben uns verfahren (driving)

Slow the car down
Fahren Sie langsamer

Can you drive faster?
Können Sie schneller fahren?

I need to get out here
Ich muss hier raus

We are looking for a gas / petrol station
Wir suchen eine Tankstelle

Can I park here?
Darf ich hier parken?

Where is the nearest parking garage?
Wo ist das nächste Parkhaus?

How long can I stay here?
Wie lange darf ich bleiben?

Where do I pay?
Wo zahle ich?

Fill the tank please
Bitte volltanken

This is my drivers license
Das ist mein Führerschein

Renting a Car and Car Trouble

We would like to rent a car
Ich möchte ein Auto mieten

We had an accident
Wir hatten einen Unfall

They have towed the car!
Sie haben das Auto abgeschleppt!

I need a tow truck
Ich brauche einen Abschleppwagen

The car has a flat tire
Das Auto hat eine Panne

The car won't start
Das Auto springt nicht an

The car has a scratch
Das Auto hat einen Kratzer

Can you recommend a garage?
Können Sie eine Werkstatt empfehlen?

Can you repair the car?
Können Sie das Auto reparieren?

How long does it take?
Wie lange dauert das

Where can I return the car?
Wo kann ich das Auto zurückbringen?

Transportation Phrases

Where is the airport?
Wo ist der Flughafen?

Where is the train station?
Wo ist der Bahnhof?

Where is the ticket machine?
Wo ist der Fahrkartenautomat?

Is that within walking distance? –-
Kann man zu Fuss gehen?

Where do I transfer?
Wo kann ich umsteigen?

How much luggage may I bring?
Wieviel Gepäck darf ich mitnehmen?

At what gate will I find the airplane?
Auf welchem Flugsteig finden wir das Flugzeug?

The flight has been delayed
Der Flug hat verspätet

Does this bus stop in Granada too?
Halt der Bus in Granada?

Is there a stopover?
Muss man umsteigen?

Is there public transportation?
Gibt es öffentliche Verbindungen?

When do we arrive?
Wann kommen wir an?

What is the name of the next station?
Wie heisst die nächste Station?

Where do we go?
Wohin fahren wir?

In the House, Friends and Guests

Guests and Invitations

Please lay the table for dinner
Bitte decke den Tisch zum Abendessen

You are invited
Sie sind eingeladen

Welcome you to our house
Willkommen in unserem Haus

Please come in
Bitte kommen sie rein

We have prepared dinner for you
Wir haben Abendessen für Sie gemacht

You can bring your family
Sie können Ihre Familie mitbringen

Tonight we are expecting guests
Heute Abend erwarten wir Gäste

I have received an invitation
Ich habe eine Einladung erhalten

We are all one family
Wir sind alle eine Familie

This is the key for the main entrance
Das sind die Schlüssel für den Haupteingang

This is the key for the room
Das sind die Schlüssel für das Zimmer

Where can we leave our luggage?
Wo können wir unser Gepäck lassen?

I would like to invite you
Ich möchte Sie einladen

We want to cancel our reservation
Wir wollen die Reservierung canceln

We are organizing a barbecue evening
Wir organisieren einen Grillabend

We have a bathroom for men and for women
Wir haben ein Bad für Männer und Frauen

Do you have a guest house?
Haben Sie ein Gästehaus?

We prefer to sleep in a private room
Wir bevorzugen in einem Privatzimmer zu schlafen

We had a great time
Wir hatten eine gute Zeit

There is no smoking in the room
Im Zimmer wird nicht geraucht

Can you please turn down the volume?
Können Sie das leiser machen?

To clean the ceiling
Die Decke reinigen

Please clean the room before you leave
Bitte reinige das Zimmer bevor du gehst

There is a cleaning fee.
Es gibt eine Reinigungsgebühr

You have damaged something
Sie haben was kaputt gemacht

Cleaning

We need a charlady / maid
Wir brauchen eine Putzfrau

Please clean the corners too
Bitte auch die Ecken saubermachen

Clean the carpet with a vacuum cleaner
Mache den Teppich mit dem Staubsauger sauber

Please clean the windows
Bitte die Fenster reinigen

Put the bottles into the refrigerator
Stell die Flaschen in den Kühlschrank

You have to make the bed too
Du musst auch das Bett machen

Can you water the plants please?
Kannst du den Pflanzen Wasser geben?

Turn down the heating
Stell die Heizung runter

Screw a new light bulb into the lamp
Schraube ein neue Glühbirne in die Lampe

To mop the floor
Den Flur wischen

Get the trash outside
Bring den Müll raus

Please empty the buckets
Leer den Eimer aus

Carry the cases into the basement
Trage die Kisten in den Keller

Clean the closets too
Mache auch die Schränke sauber

Fluff and shake the pillows
Die Kissen ausschütteln

Close the shutters
Die Jalousienen schließen

Don't forget to lock the doors
Vergiss nicht die Türen zu schließen

Household Chores

To paint the wall
Die Wand malen

Roll up the carpets!
Den Teppich aufrollen

The bathroom needs to be cleaned
Das Badezimmer muss gereinigt werden

Polish the mirrors too
Poliere auch die Spiegel

You are not allowed to make a break / no pause
Pausen sich nicht erlaubt

We pay once a month
Wir zahlen einmal im Monat

Open all the windows
Öffne alle Fenster

We appreciate your good work
Wir schätzen Ihre Arbeit

Housekeeping
Haushalt / Zimmerreinigung (Hotel)

Business, Renting and Real Estate

Business and Negotiations

I need a receipt / bill
Ich brauche eine Rechnung

I am interested
Ich bin interessiert

Thank's, but I am not interested
Danke, aber ich bin nicht interessiert

I want to speak with the owner!
Ich will mit dem Besitzer sprechen!

I the price negotiable?
Ist der Preis verhandelbar?

This is my team
Das ist meine Mannschaft

We make a contract
Wir machen einen Vertrag

We pay later
Wir zahlen patter

We order tomorrow
Wir bestellen morgen

When can you deliver?
Wann können Sie liefern?

Who is paying customs?
Wer zahlt den Zoll?

How much are the total costs?
Wie hoch sind die Gesamtkosten?

What is your best price?
Was ist ihr bester Preis?

We want to cancel
Wir wollen stornieren

It is too expensive
Es ist zu teuer

Are taxes included?
Sind Steuern inbegriffen?

How much is the commission?
Wie hoch ist die Kommission?

I need to write it down
Ich muss das aufschreiben

I need this in writing
Ich brauche das schriftlich

What are the delivery terms?
Wie sind die Lieferbedingungen?

Does this product has warranties?
Hat das Produkt Garantie?

Will you accept the order?
Werden Sie die Bestellung akzeptieren?

We make you an offer
Wir machen Ihnen ein Angebot

We accept your offer
Wir akzeptieren Ihr Angebot

We reject your offer
Wir lehnen Ihr Angebot ab

We pay after delivery
Wir zahlen nach der Lieferung

We pay now
Wir zahlen jetzt

Is there a discount?
Gibt es Rabatt? / Skonto?

Do you accept credit cards?
Akzeptieren Sie Kreditkarten?

Banking Phrases and Terms

I am looking for an ATM
Ich suche einen Geldautomaten

Do they change dollar?
Werden Dollar gewechselt?

I'd like to open a checking account
Ich möchte ein Girokonto eröffnen

I like to open a savings account.
Ich möchte ein Sparkonto eröffnen

What documents do I need?
Welche Dokumente brauche ich?

The ATM machine did not dispense notes
Der Geldautomat hat kein Geld ausgegeben

I want to apply for a personal credit
Ich möchte einen Privatkredit beantragen

I want to cash a cheque
Ich möchte einen Scheck wechseln

I need cash money from my account
Ich brauche Bargeld von meinem Konto

Insurance -- Phrases and Terms

Do you have insurance?
Sind Sie versichert?

Is your car insured
Ist Ihr Auto versichert?

Do you have accident insurance?
Sind sie gegen Unfall versichert?

We would like to insure the car
Wir möchten das Auto versichern

I need a household insurance
Ich brauche eine Hausratversicherung

Let me get my insurance papers
Lassen Sie mich die Versicherungs Papiere holen

I have everything insured
Ich habe alles versichert

We should file the police report
Wir sollten einen Polizeireport aufnehmen

We should file a damage report
Wir sollten einen Schadensreport aufnehmen

Are they going to raise our premiums?
Werden sie unsere Prämien erhöhen?

We don't agree with appraisal
Wir glauben nicht an die Einschätzung

I am the beneficiary
Ich bin der Begünstigte

We need a free tariff
Wir brauchen einen kostenfreien Tarif

Where can I buy a car insurance
Wo kann ich eine Autoversicherung kaufen?

I need a health insurance
Ich brauche eine Krankenversicherung

We'd like to insure our property
Wir wollen unser Eigentum versichern

Can we pay by annual installments?
Kann man jährlich zahlen?

How much are the deductibles?
Wieviel sind die Abschreibungen

I need a travel insurance.
Ich brauche eine Reiseversicherung

Signing of a contract
Vertragsunterzeichnung

I need a life insurance
Ich brauche eine Lebensversicherung

Real Estate – Phrases and Terms

What kind of neighbors do we have here?
Welche Art Nachbarn haben wir hier?

When was this house built?
Wann wurde das Haus gebaut?

How much is the property / land tax?
Wie hoch sind die Grundsteuern?

How much are the running costs ?
Wie hoch sind die laufenden Kosten?

We would like to view the house
Wir möchten das Haus besichtigen

Are you the owner of this property?
Sie Sie der Hauseigentümer?

Is this house rented?
Ist das Haus vermietet?

Who is living in this house?
Wer lebt im Haus?

Is there a community pool?
Gibt es ein Gemeinde Schwimmbecken?

How much is the administration fee?
Wie hoch sind die Wohngebühren?

How many square meters has the land?
Wieviel Quadratmeter hat das Land?

How many floors has this house?
Wie viele Stockwerke hat das Haus?

This house needs to be renovated
Das Haus muss renoviert werden

How many people are registered in the deed?
Wie viele Personen sind im Grundbuch eingetragen?

Do you have a floor plan?
Haben Sie einen Grundriss?

Is this house owned by the bank?
Gehört das Haus der Bank?

We don't need a realtor / broker
Wir brauchen keinen Makler

Is the house rented?
Ist das Haus vermietet?

Do you offer financing?
Bieten Sie Finanzierung an?

Legal Terms and Situations

the deed / title (real estate)
das Grundbuch

the contract
der Vertrag

Real estate contracts are signed by a notary
Immobilien Verträge werden beim Notar unterzeichnet

To pay a deposit
Eine Anzahlung zahlen

It's already confirmed
Es ist schon konfirmiert

the witness
der Zeuge

the judge
der Richter

to denounce
anzeigen

criminal charges
Anklagepunkte

to bail someone
eine Kaution hinterlegen

You are accused of...
Sie werden beschuldigt...

a trial
die Gerichtsverhandlung

I have to go to court
Ich muss zu Gericht

Lawyer's fee
Anwaltshonorar

State attorney
Staatsanwalt

We need a translator
Wir brauchen einen Übersetzer

Do I have to pay a fine?
Muss ich eine Strafe bezahlen?

We need a lawyer
Wir brauchen einen Rechtsanwalt

Is it against the law?
Verstößt es gegen ein Gesetz?

What are the legal requirements?
Was sind die legalen Voraussetzungen?

We would like to register
Wir möchten uns anmelden

What is my legal status?

Was ist mein legaler Status?

Who has the custody?
Wer hat das Sorgerecht?

I am not guilty
Ich bin unschuldig

I will sue you for fraud
Ich werde Sie wegen Betrug verklagen

Education, at Work and Sports

Education and University

Where can I register?
Wo kann ich mich registrieren?

When is semester break?
Wann sind Semesterferien?

What is your principle area of study?
Was ist dein Studienfach?

When is the examen
Wann ist Examen?

Let's go to the university!
Laß uns zur Universität gehen!

What is the campus policy?
Was ist die Kampus Ordnung?

How much is the fee?
Wieviel kosten die Studiengebühren?

Are there still enrollment places available?
Gibt es noch Studienplätze?

What are the degree courses?
Welche Fachkurse werden angeboten?

Do they offer financial aid?
Wird Studienfinanzierung angeboten?

What major degrees do they offer?
Welche Studienabschlüsse werden angeboten?

Where can I study?
Wo kann ich studieren?

Is the food in the canteen edible?
Ist das Essen in der Mensa geniessbar?

Where can I get the learning material?
Wo bekomme ich das Studienmaterial?

I meet you in the auditorium
Ich treffe dich im Auditorium

his university has an entrance examination
Diese Universität hat ein Einschreibungs-Verfahren

At Work

He / she is calling
Er / Sie ruft an

I'd like to speak with Mr./Ms. ….
Ich möchte gern Herrn/Frau…sprechen.

The line is busy
Die Leitung ist besetzt

What time suits you?
Wann passt es Ihnen?

Can I have a receipt please?
Kann ich bitte eine Rechnung haben?

My boss said ...
Mein Chef / meine Chefin hat gesagt, …

I need a copy
Ich brauche eine Kopie

Did I get mail?
Habe ich Post bekommen?

I'd like to make an appointment
I möchte einen Termin machen

Can we meet on Thursday morning?
Können wir uns Donnerstag morgens treffen?

This is part of my job
Das ist Teil meiner Arbeit

This is not a problem at all!
Das ist überhaupt kein Problem!

I have already finished my work
Ich bin schon mit meiner Arbeit fertig!

Have a nice trip / a good vacation
Schönen Urlaub!

Sports

We like soccer
Wir mögen Fußball

When does the game start?
Wann fängt das Spiel an?

Are you a fan of...?
Bist du ein Fan von..?

Can we join the group?
Können wir diese Gruppe beitreten?

We like sports
Wir mögen Sport

We play a game
Wir spielen ein Spiel

Where can we rent a bicycle?
Wo können wir ein Fahrrad mieten?

Is there a gym here?
Gibt es hier ein Fitness Center?

How much is membership?
Wieviel kostet eine Mitgliedschaft?

I need to make exercise to lose weight
Ich muss Sport machen um abzunehmen

I like to play tennis
Ich mag Tennis spielen

I like to swim
Ich mag schwimmen

I am looking for a yoga group
Ich suche eine Yoga Gruppe

I try to find a fitness instructor
Ich versuche einen Fitness Lehrer zu finden

Can you help me to lift the weights?
Kannst du mir helfen die Gewichte zu heben?

I need aerobics
Ich brauche Aerobics / Cardio

I have to start slowly
Ich muss langsam anfangen

We are looking for a good diving spot
Wir suchen einen guten Tauchplatz

Small Talk and Entertainment

Talk About Yourself

What is your profession?
Was machen Sie beruflich

I work for the … company
Ich arbeiter bei der...Firma

I have my own business
Ich bin selbständig

I am employed
Ich bin angestellt

I am a student
Ich bin Student

I am a Chemist
Ich bin Chemiker

I live alone
Ich lebe allein

I have two children
Ich habe zwei Kinder

I am married
Ich bin verheiratet

Where do you live
Wo leben Sie / Wo lebst du?

Do you have an address?
Haben Sie / hast du eine Adresse?

I live in Berlin
Ich wohne in Berlin

Do you live in Hamburg?
Wohnen Sie / wohnst du in Hamburg?

Tomorrow we have a party
Morgen machen wir eine Party

Do you have siblings
Haben Sie / Hast du Geschwister?

Shall I bring something?
Soll ich was mitbringen?

May I bring my dog?
Darf ich meinen Hund mitbringen?

We have a house in the center
Wir haben ein Haus im Zentrum

Trivial Conversation Phrases for Travelers

Where are you going?
Wohin gehst du?

Are you here on holidays?
Bist du auf Urlaub hier?

I would like to invite you
Ich würde dich gerne einladen

It doesn't matter
Es macht nichts

We are just passing through
Wir sind auf der Durchreise

I can cook for you
Ich kann für dich kochen

It will be good
Es wird gut sein

Do you know..?
Wissen Sie? / Weisst du?

I can help you
Ich kann dir / Ihnen helfen

I am good at it
Damit bin ich gut

I need a protection suntan cream
Ich brauche Sonnenschutz Kräme

What is your favorite color?
Was ist deine Lieblingsfarbe?

come / come along
Komm mit

Can I join you?
Darf ich mitkommen?

Please wait here
Bitte warten Sie hier

This is forbidden!
Das ist verboten!

Can I smoke here?
Darf man hier rauchen

Do you have a question?
Haben Sie eine Frage?

Do you mind if I..?
Stört es Sie, wenn ich…?

Let's do it together!
Lasst uns es gemeinsam machen

Let's celebrate!
Lasst uns feiern!

Entertainment and Recreation

Tonight we go out
Heute Abend gehen wir aus

We go to a concert
Wir gehen in ein Konzert

How much are the tickets?
Wie viel kosten die Karten?

We will meet at the entrance
Wir treffen uns am Eingang

What movie will we watch?
Welchen Film arden wir sehen?

Did you like the movie?
Gefiel Ihnen der Film? / Gefiel dir der Film?

Is there a good night club?
Gibt es einen guten Nachtclub?

Do you like dancing?
Magst du tanzen?

Can I go with you?
Darf ich mitkommen?

This is fun!
Das macht Spass!

This is boring.
Das ist langweilig

Are you coming with me?
Kommst du mit?

Do they have a botanical garden here?
Gibt es einen Botanisches Garten hier?

Is there a public swimming pool?
Gibt es ein öffentliches Schwimmbad?

Which museum can you recommend?
Welches Museum können Sie empfehlen?

We are looking for a spa
Wir suchen eine Sauna

Where can I get a massage?
Wo kann ich eine Massage bekommen?

Is the movie in original language?
Ist der Film in original Sprache?

Orders

Stop! / Hold it!
Stehenbleiben!

Hurry up!
Beeilung!

Wait here
Warten Sie hier / Warte hier

What are you dong?
Was machen Sie?

Go on!
Weiter!

Achtung!
Attention!

Get out of here!
Verschwinden Sie / Verschwinde!

How dare you?
Wie können Sie es wagen? / Wie kannst du es wagen?

Come on!
Komm schon!

Later
Später

Drive on
Weiterfahren

Holidays, Seaons, Christmas and Signs

Seasons and Festivals

the seasons
die Jahreszeiten

spring
das Frühjahr

summer
der Sommer

autumn
der Herbst

winter
der Winter

January
Januar

February
Februar

March
März

April
April

May
May

June
Juni

July
July

August
August

September
September

October
Oktober

November
November

December
Dezember

Public Holidays and Terms for Vacations

January 1, New Year's Day
Neujahr

Beginning of holidays
Urlaubsanfang

Main vacation season
Hauptreisezeit

Short trip
Kurzreise

Long trips, permanent travelers
Langzeitreisende

Holidays / vacation
Ferien / Urlaub

Corpus Christi Day
Fronleichnam (Catholic States)

15 August, Assumption
Wiederauferstehung (Catholic States)

1. May
Tag der Deutschen Arbeit

1 November, All saints Day
Allerheiligen

Oktoberfest
Oktoberfest
Most of the festivals are taken place in Bavaria, starting 2st week in September

8. December Reunification (Germany)
Wiedervereinigung

24. December Holy Night
Heilige Nacht

25. December, Christmas Day
Weihnachten

Christmas Phrases

We are looking for a Christmas gift
Wir suchen ein Weihnachtsgeschenk

Where are the Christmas markets?
Wo ist der Weihnachtsmarkt?

Can you wrap it up please?
Können Sie das bitte einpacken?

They don't have Santa Claus in Spain
In Spanien gibt es keinen Weihnachtsmann

We love Christmas time
Wir lieben die Weihnachtszeit

Christmas songs are important
Weihnachtslieder sind wichtig

We are looking for a Christmas tree
Wir suchen einen Weihnachtsbaum

We need help to decorate it
Wir brauchen beim Dekorieren Hilfe

We are going to visit our family for Christmas
Weihnachten besuchen wir unsere Familie

What do you have for Christmas dinner?
Was gibt e zum Weihnachtsessen?

We only go to church at Christmas
Wir gehen nur Weihnachten in die Kirche

I have a Christmas gift for you
Ich habe ein Weihnachtsgeschenk für dich

Church and Religion

We are protestants
Wir sind Protestantisch

We are catholic
Wir sind Katholisch

We are muslims
Wir sind Moslemen

We are buddhists
Wir sind Buddhisten

God is above all
Gott ist über alles

What is your believe/religion?
Was ist ihr Glaube / ihre Religion?

My religion is…
Meine Religion ist...

Do you believe in God?
Glauben Sie an Gott?

We are a very religious family
Wir sind eine religiöse Familie

We go to church on Sundays
Wir gehen Sonntags in die Kirche

At what time does the mass start?
Wann fängt die Messe an?

Where is the synagogue?
Wo ist die Synagoge?

Where is the mosque?
Wo ist die Moschee?

I would like to see a priest
Ich möchte einen Priester sehen

I would like to pray
Ich möchte beten

Let us pray together
Lasst uns zusammen beten

Religious holidays
Religiöse Feiertage

The bible is important to me
Die Bibel ist wichtig für mich

Is there a bible study group?
Gibt es eine Bibel Studiengruppe

Signs and Notices

open
offen

closed
geschlossen

hot
heiss

cold
kalt

beautiful
schon

ugly
ekelhaft

empty
leer

full
voll

new
neu

old
alt

clean
sauber

dirty
dreckig

bright
strahlend

dark
dunkel

cheap
billig

expensive
teuer

interesting
interessant

boring
langweilig

friendly
freundlich

unfriendly
unfreundlich

nice / pleasant
nett

a great time
eine tolle Zeit

lucky
Glück gehabt

bad luck
Pech gehabt

generous
großzügig

stingy
geizig

honest
ehrlich

dishonest
unehrlich

free
umsonst

for sale
zu verkaufen

to rent
zu vermieten

I agree
Ich stimme zu

Social Media, Computer and Hobbies

Can I join your group?
Darf ich der Gruppe beitreten?

Is advertising allowed?
Sind Anzeigen erlaubt?

I would like to participate
Ich würde gerne mitmachen

What are the rules for this group?
Was sind die Regeln in dieser Gruppe?

Spam is prohibited
Spam ist verboten

Can you help me to find an app auf Deutsch?
Kannst du mir helfen ein App auf Deutsch zu finden?

Can you help me to install a program?
Kannst du mir helfen ein Programm zu installieren?

I need original components
Ich brauche Original--Teile

Does it come with a cable?
Kommt es mit einem Kabel?

The printer doesn't print
Der Drucker druckt nicht

Where can I buy printer cartridges?
Wo kann ich Drucker-Patronen kaufen?

Where do they repair computers?
Wo repariert man Computers?

My tablet needs a new glass
Mein Tablet braucht ein neues Glass

Where can I download this?
Wo kann ich das runterladen?

Arts & Hobbies

Where is the museum?
Wo ist das Museum?

This is magnificent
Das ist großartig

Who built all of this?
Wer hat das alles gebaut?

What's the name of the artist?
Wie heisst der Künstler?

We appreciate art
Wir schätzen Kunst

Do you know the artist?
Kennen Sie den Kunstler?

How did you clean the sculpture?
Wie haben Sie die Skulptur gereinigt??

This is a beautiful painting
Das ist ein schönes Bild

How old is it?
Wie alt ist das?

Does it have a signature?
Ist es signiert?

This is rare
Das ist selten

What's the name of this style?
Wie arde dieser Stil?

Are you an expert?
Sind Sie ein Experte?

We are only interested in authentic arts
Wir sind nur an authentischer Kunst interessiert

This is only of personal value
Das hat nur einen persönlichen Wert

Is this original?
Ist es original?

Words and Phrases for Kids

yes
ja

no
nein

Hello!
Hallo!

Thank you
Danke

Thank you very much!
Vielen Dank!

Excuse me
Entschuldigung

Do speak English?
Sprechen Sie Englisch? / Sprichst du Englisch?

Do you speak German?
Sprechen Sie Deutsch? / Sprichst du Deutsch?

My name is Elli.
Ich heisse Elli.

That's a nice name.
Das ist ein schöner Name.

Thanks. See you later.
Danke. Bis später

Bye
Tschüss

Goodbye
Auf Wiedersehen

Good morning
Guten Morgen

Good evening
Guten Abend

Good night
Gute Nacht

I am hungry
Ich habe Hunger.

I am thirsty
Ich habe Durst

Are you hungry?
Hast du Hunger?

Would you like to have…?
Möchtest du ...?

Do you like ice cream?
Magst du Eis?

Do you like to go to the movies / cinema?
Möchtest du ins Kino?

The circus
Der Zirkus

The playground
Der Spielplatz

Where is our car?
Wo steht unser Auto?

Where does it hurt?
Wo tut es weh?

Where do you go?
Wohin gehst du?

I would like to stay.
Ich möchte bleiben.

I need to know….
Ich muss wissen…

I need to talk to someone.
Ich muss mit jemanden reden.

I need to go to the bathroom.
Ich muss auf die Toilette.

Do you have to go the bathroom?
Musst du auf die Toilette gehen?

Do you want to go home?
Möchtest du nach Hause?

Do you want to play a game?
Möchtest du ein Spiel spielen?

Your toys
Dein Spielzeug

We take the train.
Wir nehmen den Zug.

We ride the bike.
Wir fahren mit dem Fahrrad.

What is your favorite color?
Was ist deine Lieblingsfarbe?

blue
blau

red
rot

yellow
gelb

green
grün

white
weiß

black
schwarz

pink
rosa

brown
braun

I understand.
Ich verstehe.

I don’t understand.
Ich verstehe nicht.

Help!
Hilfe!

***

www.ingramcontent.com/pod-product-compliance
Lightning Source LLC
Chambersburg PA
CBHW061610190726
48288CB00007B/2259

* 9 7 8 1 9 9 9 3 5 3 0 7 0 *